PARANORMAL BUCKINGHAMSHIRE

EDDIE BRAZIL

AMBERLEY

First published 2023

Amberley Publishing
The Hill, Stroud
Gloucestershire, GL5 4EP

www.amberley-books.com

British Library Cataloguing in Publication Data.
A catalogue record for this book is available from the British Library.

ISBN 978 1 3981 1465 4 (print)
ISBN 978 1 3981 1466 1 (ebook)

Typesetting by SJmagic DESIGN SERVICES, India.
Printed in Great Britain.

Contents

Introduction

Ghost. What an enigmatic word. For over 2,000 years ghosts have continued to baffle, puzzle and fascinate mankind, yet in today's computer- and mobile phone-obsessed world the true nature of those things which go bump in the night still evades scientific scrutiny. The Oxford English Dictionary defines the word 'ghost' as the disembodied soul of a dead person haunting the living. This description would conveniently fit most people's idea of the archetypal spook; a phantom which walks or glides the midnight corridors of stately mansions or romantic castles, or for the purpose of this book, spectres which roam the county of Buckinghamshire and are completely unaware of being viewed by trembling spectators.

However, years of research by psychical investigators have revealed that there are numerous paranormal manifestations of what we would normally term a 'ghost'. They include poltergeists, crisis apparitions, stone tape apparitions, atmospheric photographic ghosts, historical ghosts, and the curious enigma of phantoms of the living. All have their own peculiarities and ways of manifesting their presence or energy.

If they have all got one thing in common it is their rejection by established science as proof of an afterlife, and are looked upon as preternatural phenomena which will eventually be shown, by scientific means, to have a rational and logical explanation.

What *have* been established over the years are a number of theories as to what ghosts could be. Despite their skepticism, a minority of scientists are willing to accept that some types of poltergeist phenomena, which involves the movement of objects and the typically associated raps, bumps and knocks, if not fraud, is psychokinetic in nature – i.e., mind over matter – and is possibly due to the subconscious manifestation of the pent-up sexual frustration and aggression of a disturbed adolescent.

Historical ghosts which repeat the same actions over and over are viewed as psychic recordings which probably have their basis in the stone tape theory, a hypothesis which suggests that human trauma and emotions can imprint psychic energy within the fabric of a building. At a later date, a person possessing psychical or mediumistic abilities, on entering the building, will be able to access the imprinted energy and, acting somewhat like a psychic video player, replay the incident which caused the initial trauma. Depending on their own clairvoyant abilities, they will sense, hear or see incidents which have occurred previously.

The ghosts and phantoms which haunt Buckinghamshire may well be stone tape incidents. They could also be the product of an overexcited imagination, or, in some instances, even hoodwinking by practical jokers. Yet, not all can be explained away so easily. Many of the of the strange encounters contained within this book display all the hallmarks of phenomena which at the present time has no rational explanation. I hope you enjoy reading these ghostly accounts as much as I have enjoyed researching and writing them. Perhaps they will send a shiver down the spine, and hopefully make you think once again about those things which go bump in the night. As for myself, I think Shakespeare probably got it right: there are more things in heaven and earth than are dreamt of in our philosophy.

The Phantom Night Nurse

Certain places and ghosts seem to go hand in glove – castles, churches, stately homes, railways, etc. Other locations which are indisputably ripe for ghosts tales are hospitals, particularly those which were built in the Victorian era and have not undergone too much modernisation. It may seem strange to think of a hospital as a home for the paranormal, especially when one considers how busy they are during a frantic day with the public queuing and waiting for appointments, nurses and doctors hurrying between wards and a myriad of tradespeople delivering or picking up goods. The whole building can resemble the concourse of a main line station at rush hour.

However, come nightfall when the public have left, the departments are closed, the gift and paper kiosks are all locked up and there is only a handful of staff on duty to wander the dimly lit and eerily empty corridors and stairways, then the hospital takes on a whole different atmosphere, one of brooding, shadowy silence.

The following account is of a strange experience my wife, Sue, had after the birth of our daughter, Rebecca, at the Wycombe general hospital. The pregnancy had been a difficult one, and after some complications it was decided to deliver our baby by caesarean section. At 1.30 a.m. on 26 July 1985, I became a proud father. However, the challenging labour and delivery had taken their toll on Sue, and she was required to remain at the hospital for several days after.

As she recovered in bed, my wife got used to the regular routine of the hospital day. Visits by relatives, inspections by the medical staff and patients taken to other departments by porters. When night came she was grateful for the peace and quite of the darkened ward.

One night as she dozed, she watched the young night duty nurse leave the ward to attend to some hospital business. A few moments later Sue thought that she had returned, for she saw a nurse enter the ward and begin to examine one of the cots of the sleeping babies. The other mothers on the ward were also, it seemed, fast asleep. My wife, even in her half-dozed state, noticed that the other nurse was dressed differently to her colleagues. Her uniform seemed to be more old-fashioned with a long, billowing skirt, crisply starched top and a wide, wing-like hat.

After she had checked on one of the infants, she came silently over to our daughter's cot and looked down lovingly at Rebecca. Sue could not fully see the face of the nurse in the dimness of the ward; she nevertheless, in her sleepy state, half smiled up at her. After a few moments the nurse left the ward, and it was short while later that the night duty nurse returned to her desk. To my wife it all seemed like general night hospital business and she soon drifted off to sleep.

In the morning, however, Sue recalled that the nurse who had inspected Rebecca had also only examined one other cot on the ward. She wondered if there were any problems which necessitated extra examination by a senior nurse or matron. She asked the day nurse if there was anything wrong with our daughter and explained that another nurse had checked her in the night. She went on to describe her different uniform and that she appeared to be a little older, and wondered if she was a sister or matron. The day nurse was surprised. There was no other member of staff who fitted that description, and also that the hospital no longer used matrons. Sue, however, was adamant that she had seen the nurse and rejected the idea that she could have dreamed the incident.

A few days later the strange episode of my wife's night visitor began to be circulated around the ward and she was spoken to by a senior member of the nursing staff.

'I believe you and your little one were visited by our resident ghostly angel?'

Sue was puzzled

'By whom?'

'Our ghostly matron'.

The senior nurse went on to explain that it was believed that the hospital had a resident ghost who always looked in on newborn infants who had undergone a difficult birth. She was a matron back in the 1950s and although she couldn't have kids herself, always took a special interest in the well-being of children. Her presence has often been felt, and at times her ghost has been seen on the ward and throughout the hospital. My wife was taken aback to realise that the nurse she had smiled up at from her bed that night was in fact a ghost.

Of course all of this would seem to be in the realms of the fantastic. A benevolent spirit roaming the wards of a hospital late at night to keep an eye on newly born infants is just too far-fetched to be taken seriously. It would imply that ghosts are not just recordings or the product of an over-imaginative mind, but in fact spirits of dead people who are still able to act within the realm of the living. I do not doubt the veracity of my wife's experience, but a sceptic would point out that she was in a sleepy, half-awake state where our minds can play tricks. They would also point out the eerie nature of a hospital at night being an influencing factor.

Nonetheless, my wife, the nursing staff and even a few hard-headed doctors that I spoke to about the episode all attest that the hospital does indeed have not one, but at least four resident ghosts.

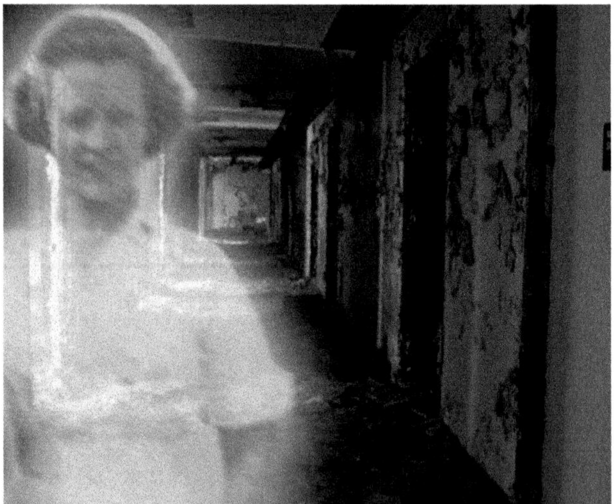

The phantom night nurse.

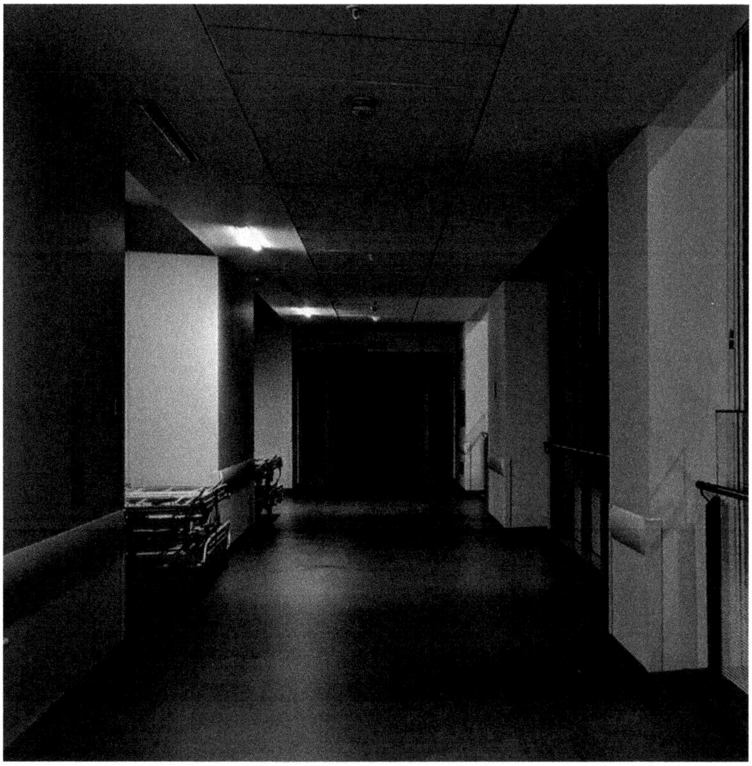

Right: Eerie hospital corridors at night.

Below: High Wycombe Hospital.

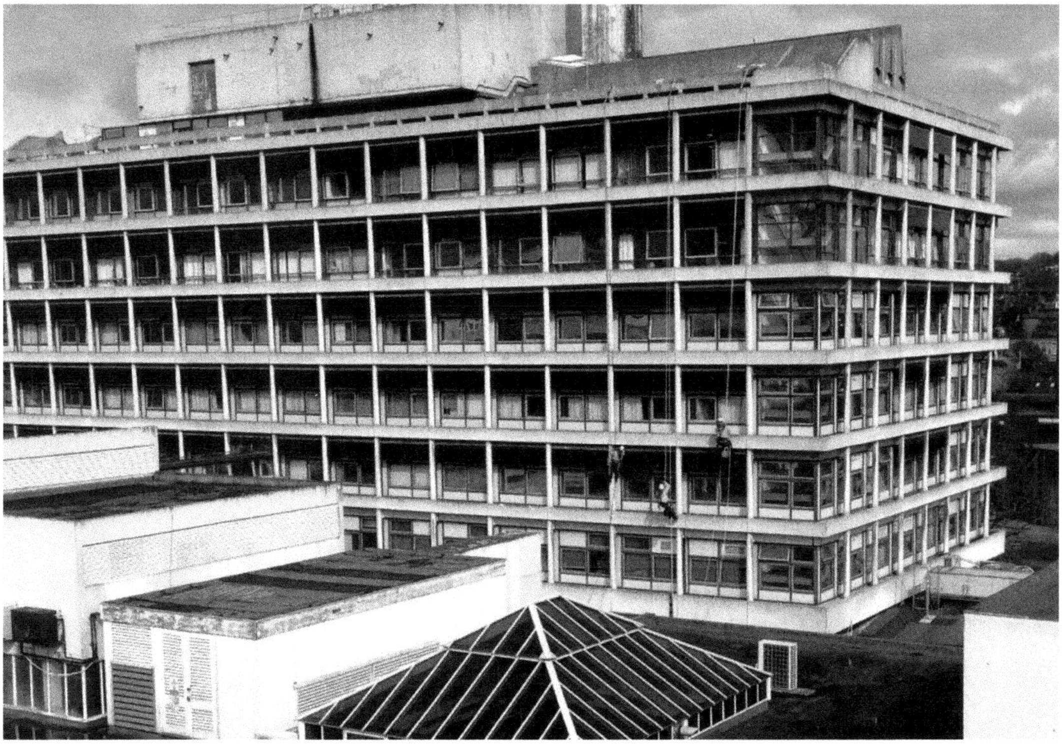

The Ghost of Ruth Ellis

The village church of Penn is located on a side road between High Wycombe and Beaconsfield, and is full of history. The grandsons of William Penn, he of Pennsylvania fame, lie in the church's vaults. Within the churchyard are the graves of David Blakeley and Donald Maclean. Blakeley was murdered by Ruth Ellis, the last woman to be hanged in Britain. Maclean gained infamy as a Soviet spy.

The church is believed to be haunted by a phantom horseman who rides through the village on moonlit nights and disappears on reaching the graveyard. A more substantial ghost is that of the apparition of a woman in white who passes through the churchyard through the east gate and vanishes down a nearby lane. In recent years some paranormal investigators have speculated that the apparition of the woman may be the spirit of Ruth Ellis. David Blakeley, a resident of Penn, and Ellis were lovers. She shot him outside a London pub in 1955. Does she return to haunt the grave of the man she said she loved?

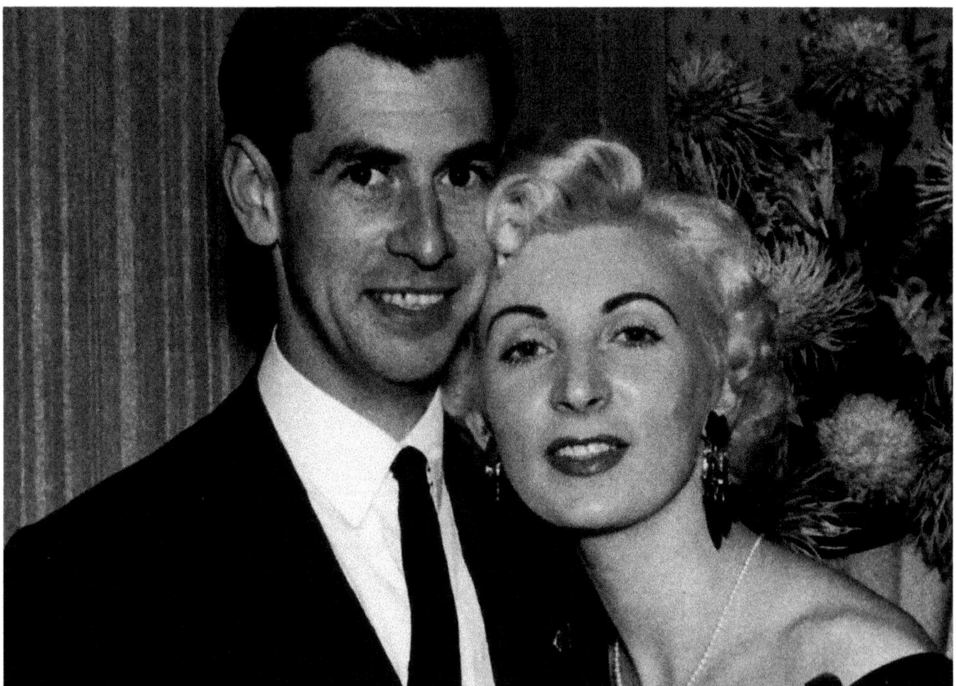

Ruth Ellis and the man she murdered, her lover David Blakeley.

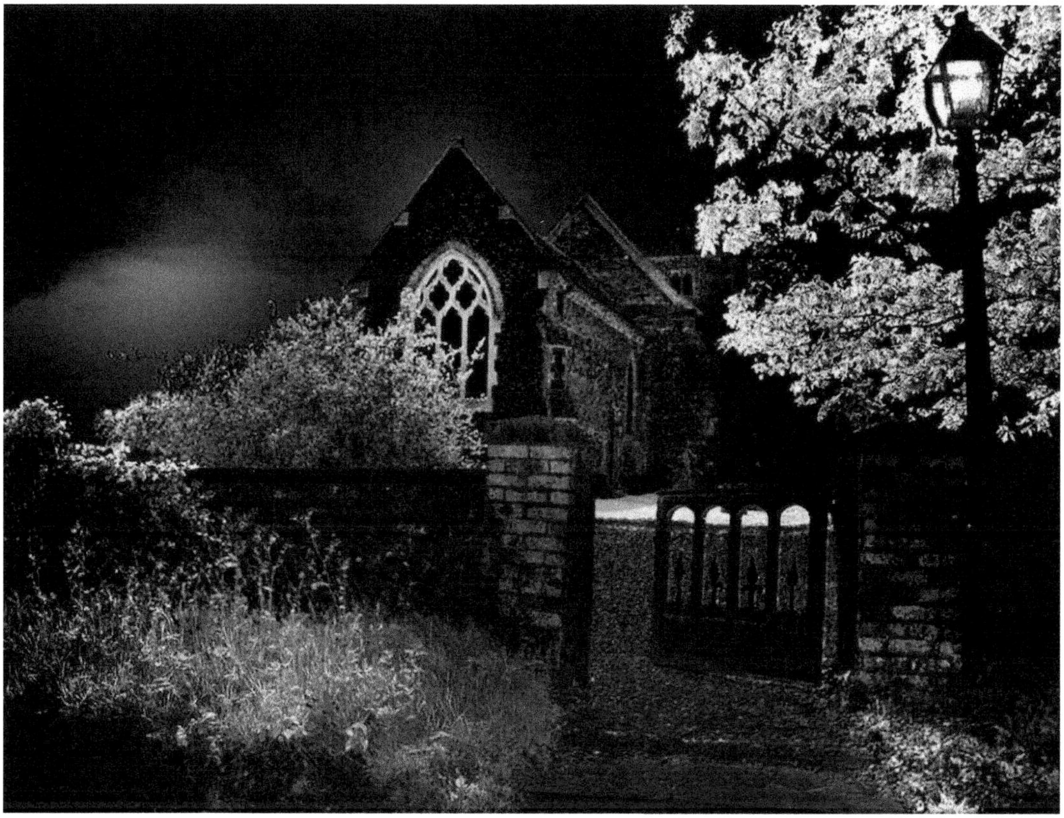

The east gate at Penn church through which the Woman in White is said to pass.

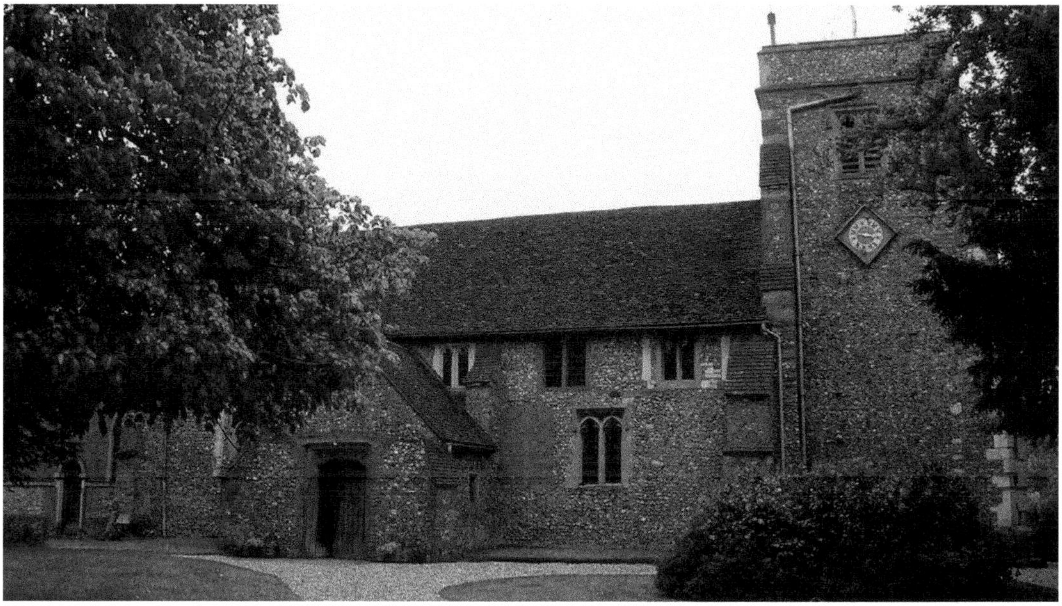

Penn church.

The Haunted Cottage

Ghosts can turn up in the most unlikely locations, yet one of the strangest scenes of a haunting has to be the spooky goings on which occurred in an ordinary public convenience in Aylesbury and its eventual outcome within the home of a corrupt ex-police officer.

Prior to 1967 homosexuality in Britain was a crime punishable by imprisonment. Consequently, gay men had by necessity to conduct their forbidden liaisons in as discreet locations as they could find, many of which included public toilets.

In 1965, David Harris [alias] was thirty-eight, and even though he was married, had finally come out, to himself at least, and accepted that he was gay.

He worked as a barman, and from his gay friends learnt that one could enjoy a brief, no- questions-asked liaison in a local public convenience in Aylesbury or High Wycombe. Because of their Tudor/Bethan design of quaint half-timber construction, one originally found in London, the toilets were colloquially known as cottages, even though some of them were modern in design.

Harris was appalled at the idea of seeking enjoyment in such an unsavoury and public place. Yet, given the prevailing social climate at the time, and threat of jail for his sexuality if discovered, such places provided much-needed discreetness.

The routine was to wait outside the convenience and catch the eye of a receptive man. Both would descend the steps to the toilet and enter one of the cubicles for the briefest activity, and afterwards leave separately.

Harris, although apprehensive about the whole idea, nonetheless went ahead. But after waiting for some time outside no other person arrived at the toilet or left. Intrigued, he went down to the convenience, but found it empty. He wasn't surprised. It was a dimly lit, shadowy, marbled room with cracked mirrors and dripping taps. An odour of disinfectant and cheap aftershave pervaded the cold of the urinals and cubicles – the worst place for the briefest of intimate contact.

Yet there was something else which made Harris want to leave. Within there was a feeling of utter dread and unease, as if he were being watched by unseen eyes. He could understand why no one would want to spend any time in such a place. He quickly left.

Back at the bar his friends asked how he got on, and were intrigued by his experience. There were also others who confirmed his view of the cottage. One veteran of the community added to the picture: 'You wont find me trolling in that place, dear. Its not who joins you at the urinal you have to worry about, its the feeling of someone standing behind you that gives you the willies.'

All who had visited the toilet maintained the view that, even though they found it empty, there always seemed to be someone, or something in one of the cubicles.

Eventually, Harris was to learn of an event which went some way to explaining the atmosphere of the cottage.

Two years earlier in 1963 a young gay man was found dead in one of the cubicles. It was assumed that his fatal head injuries were the result of him being drunk and cracking his head on the toilet marble. Yet many in the community knew otherwise.

Allegedly, a homophobic detective constable had it in for 'queers'. He would wait outside the cottages and, acting as 'agent provocateur', entice men down in to one of the cubicles. During the act instead of arresting the man for indecency he would assault him. One night in 1963 he went too far.

It would seem, however, that the police officer eventually had his nemesis to answer to. Sometime in 1966 he was found dead in his Aylesbury flat. He lay in bed asphyxiated, but there were no strangle marks on his neck. Retribution, whether divine, paranormal or physically real was meted out to him. A piece of meat was found lodged in his throat. The detective was himself homosexual, yet hid his sexuality by his violent conduct to other gay men.

The cottage has long gone, replaced by inner-city development. One wonders if the murdered man has now found peace, or does his ghost still wander the streets of Aylesbury looking for company.

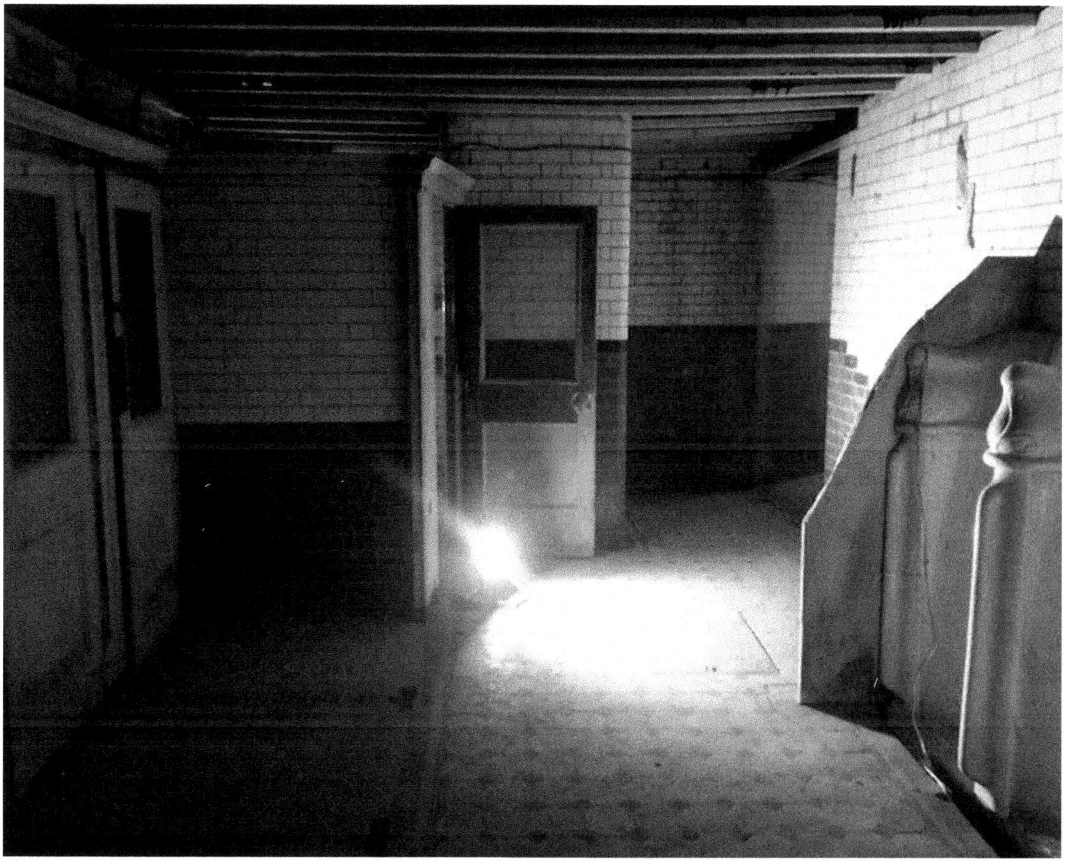

The haunted cottage.

Psycho-sexiness

The actions of a poltergeist are probably the most common reported paranormal phenomena of the modern era. It is reckoned that within a 10-mile radius of where you are reading this some form of poltergeist activity is, or has, taken place.

The noisy or banging ghost is probably the one aspect of psychic phenomena which scientists and parapsychologists are prepared to put on the table for discussion simply because they view the poltergeist as neither ghost or supernatural entity, but rather the unconscious manifestation of a person's mind – usually a disturbed or sexually frustrated female.

In 1996 Mary Windsor [alias], a fifty-two-year-old single woman, was living alone in a comfortable flat in Aylesbury in Buckinghamshire. Her plain looks and plump appearance, together with a shy demeanor, had left her without many male friends or admirers.

It was a situation which did not bother her unduly or play on her mind. She knew her worth as a person, and accepted that the right companion would one day show up.

She nonetheless, like most of us, desired the pleasure of sexual contact. At night, alone in her bed, this need would become a frustrating yearning. The longing was relieved by her own intimate means.

On one lonely night her arousal became so intense that she thought her neighbour was complaining about the yelps and cries emanating from her mouth. Yet it was more than Mary's climatic moans, for from the walls came the sound of thuds and bangs.

At once Mary stopped her pleasure to listen up. Yet, almost simultaneously so did the sounds of the banging. She obviously assumed that her silence had the desired effect and her neighbour had stopped complaining.

Over time she became more puzzled when, as she pleased herself, the banging sounds became more and more persistent. Even more alarming was the knowledge that her neighbour was away and his flat was empty. Mary believed that her home was in some way haunted.

In time she met a man who would become her partner; a plain, introverted person who nevertheless suited her. Despite their mutual reservedness, both were passionate lovemakers. Yet just as before, when Mary was reaching a climax the banging and thudding would start up. Also objects within the bedroom would jump and fly across the floor.

It now dawned on Mary that it was she herself who was causing the strange phenomena; some peculiar aberration of her mind was causing the disturbances. Fortunately for her, her partner was understanding and comforting. Research by both shed some light on the weird happenings.

A leakage of psychokinetic energy during orgasm was the nearest they could come to an answer, and even this explanation was just a theory.

Mary eventually married her partner. As the years progressed and the initial flames of passion cooled as both settled in to the mundaneness of married life, the instances of noisy sounds during lovemaking became less and less until they eventually ceased altogether.

The Ghostly Gropers of the West Wycombe Caves

In the early 1980s a lady friend of the Dashwood family was visiting West Wycombe Park and asked if she could see the infamous Hell Fire Caves. The sixty-year-old spinster was keen to see where Sir Francis Dashwood and his cronies had enjoyed their drunken orgies.

She had been told of the ghosts and phantoms which were said to wander the passageways of the labyrinth, but she dismissed this obvious attempt to dissuade her from entering the caves and brushed it aside with a laugh and added that she would walk the darkened passages alone armed only with a torch.

She was, by all accounts, a fiery woman not given to flights of fancy. She had remained unmarried and had always eschewed the company and pleasure of many male admirers. In fact it seemed she was something of a prude.

As the lady proceeded into the caves she soon reached what is known as the banqueting hall, a vast cavern carved out of the chalk and used by the members of the Hell Fire Club for their drunken dinners. It was also the place where the members practised their 'devotions' with their female companions.

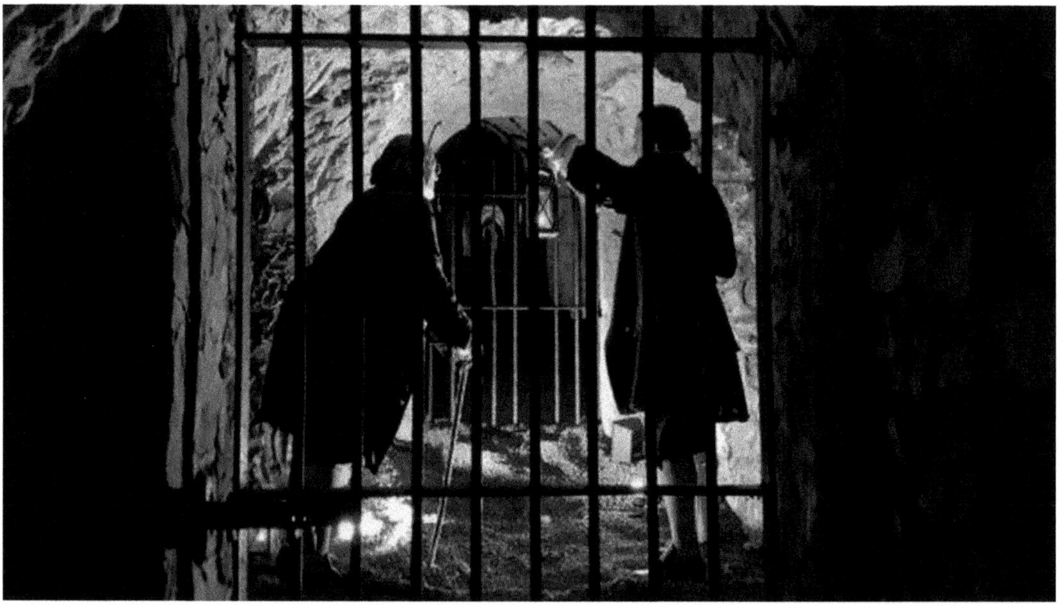

Did the ghostly members of the Hell Fire Club assault a curious lady?

As the fearless spinster looked about her she had a most, and one might say, life-changing experience. In the shadowy dark, and without warning, she says she had the unmistakable sensation of countless invisible hands touching, caressing and fondling her body in a most amorous and sensual fashion.

From head to foot the unseen hands explored her plump, curvy figure, probing in places which the good lady had never before been prodded.

Terrified, she at once fled shrieking from the chamber and back to the exit. Never again would she venture into such an evil, immoral and Godless place.

However, some years later, it became known to the Dashwoods that following the spinster's frightening but sensual encounter in the caves, a change had come over her. Whether it was the randy attentions of the ghost of Sir Francis Dashwood or the drunken lecherous groping of his phantom disciples, we will never know.

Totally out of character, the spinster decided to thrust off her prudish shackles and disdain for the pleasures of the flesh and began to court the friendship of male companions. Three score years of celibacy were abandoned as a dormant sexual awakening took place and she became a raving nymphomaniac.

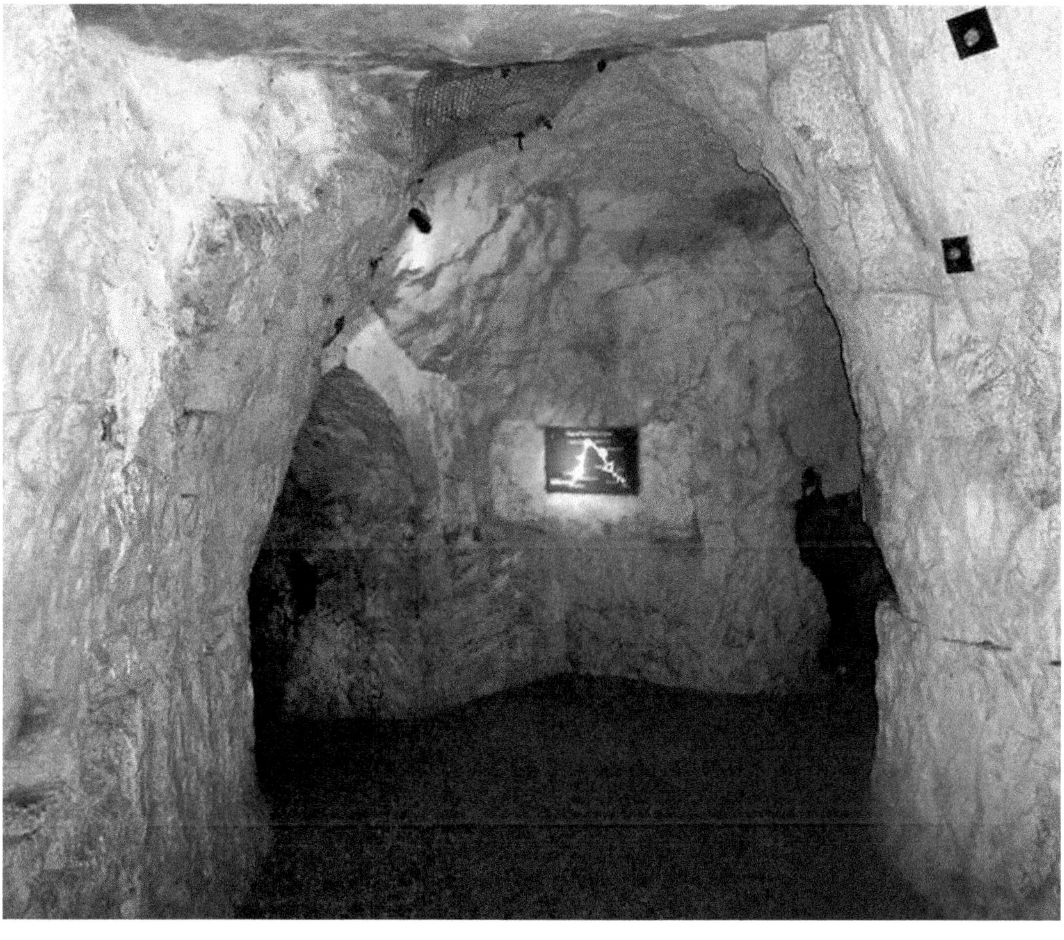

The haunted Hell Fire Caves.

The Dwarf

His name was Albert Constantine and he lived in a run-down terraced cottage opposite the Rye common in the centre of Wycombe.

A balding, fifty-eight-year-old odd job man, his diminutive stature of only 5 feet 3 inches, shuffling, awkward style of walking and an oversized, hooded duffle coat earned him the nickname Albert the Dwarf from the locals.

When the funfair made its regular twice-yearly visit to the Rye, Constantine would find work on the dodgems or ghost train.

To all who barely knew him he was a harmless, jovial soul. Yet there was another side to the Wycombe dwarf, much darker and secretive.

His offers to the youngsters of the area to return with him to his house for lemonade and sweets were eagerly accepted until stories began to circulate of the friendly arm around the kids' shoulders and the playful slap on their backside became something more sinister.

One night in 1974 Constantine was offered work on the funfair ghost train. He entered the haunted tunnel to clean it followed by three tattooed men and was never seen alive again.

Six months later Constantine's body was dragged from the Thames near Maidenhead. The funfair moved on, and the dwarf was soon un-mourned and forgotten, that is until the late 1980s.

His former home had been snapped up by eager young professionals keen to get on the property ladder. A young female city bank dealer moved in in Autumn 1988. One month later she fled the house vowing never to return.

Returning home after midnight, tired, she never gave another thought to the little figure who always stood on the Rye staring at her home. Perhaps he was homeless. Yet the young woman began to feel somewhat uncomfortable when the figure of the little man began to stare up at her bedroom window. He would at one moment be in sight and then gone.

Things took a more sinister turn when she began to experience nightmares in which the dwarf-like figure would appear in her bedroom. Each subsequent bad dream had the man moving closer to her bed. The climax came when the woman awoke in the small hours and had the terrifying sensation that there was someone in bed with her. She could feel foetid breath on her hair and the sensation of a body pressing against her back, and in an aroused state, literally paralysed with fear. She assumed that an intruder had entered her house and was now in the throes of assaulting her. She managed to scream out in terror and leapt from the bed. Running out into the street, she began howling blue murder, and soon her neighbours came to her aid.

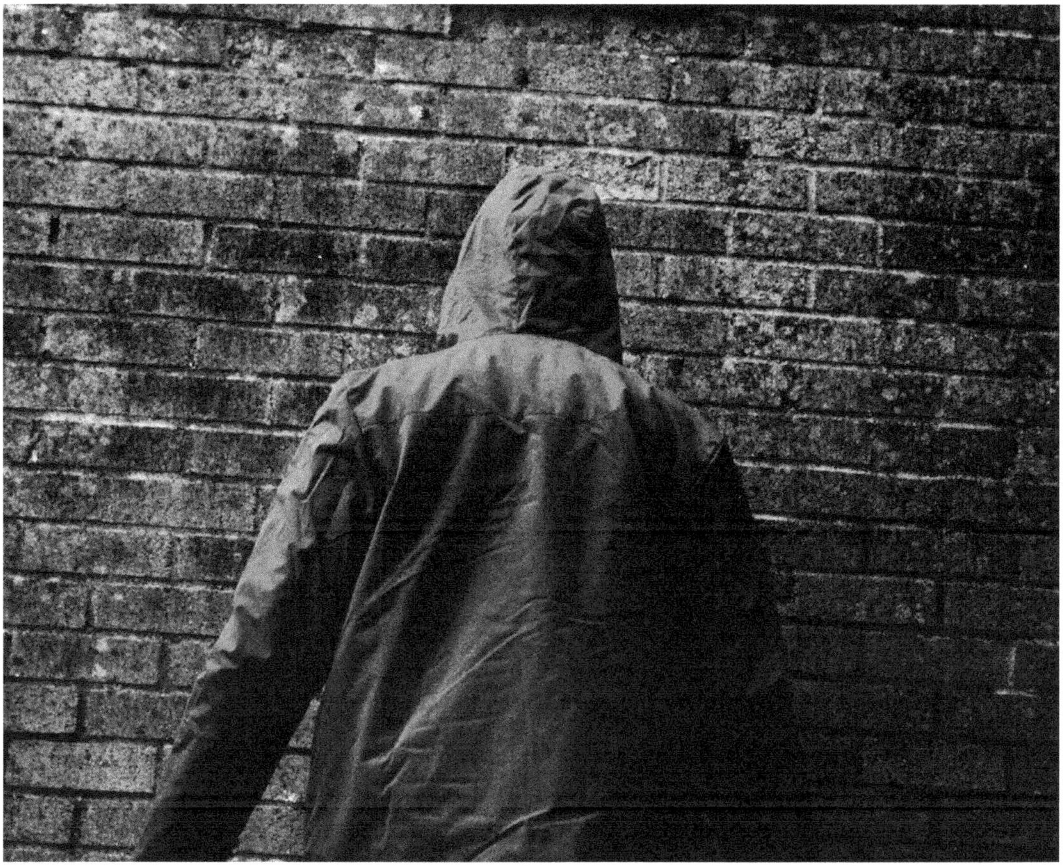

The dwarf.

Her hysterical cries that there was a man in her room prompted an immediate search by two men – they found nothing.

The woman soon moved on when she was informed of the former resident of her home and the unsavoury stories about him. The dwarf's old home has since been demolished, yet it is believed that his ghost still wanders the area; a shuffling, hooded apparition stalking the deserted lamp-lit streets of Wycombe in search of the unwary and vulnerable.

The Ghostly Vicar of Aston Sandford

Aston Sandford lies some 6 miles to the south-west of Aylesbury. It is a peaceful cul de sac hamlet in the water meadows of the Thame Valley with a tiny thirteenth-century tower-less church and a handful of cottages. Thomas Scott, grandfather of architect Giles Gilbert Scott, was vicar between 1803 and 1821, and it's his ghost that is said to haunt the church and graveyard.

Between October 1996 and March 1997, a young female commercial artist took a short let on one of the village cottages. She had the pleasure of working from home, and after a tiring day at her easel would often take a walk through the village up to the Aylesbury road.

On several occasions she tried to take a look inside the church, but found it locked. One cold November afternoon as it was approaching dusk she took here regular stroll and looking over at the church was pleased to see the vicar by the south door.

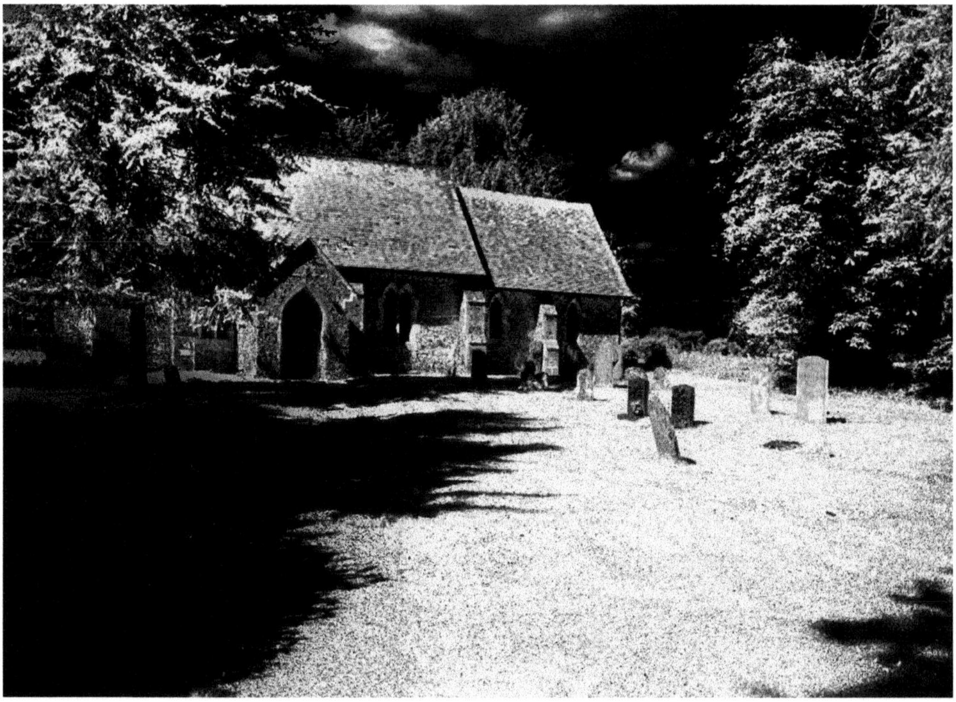

Haunted Aston Sandford church.

She decided on her return she would go over and have a look inside. Yet when she returned to the building she found it in darkness and with no sign of the vicar. Assuming that he must have finished his business quickly and locked up, she carried on home.

On several subsequent occasions she again saw the clergyman by the church, yet every time she returned to look at the building he was nowhere to be seen and the church appeared empty. The young woman was by now becoming a little curious about the vicar's behaviour. On her next walk she decided if she saw him she would go over immediately and introduce herself.

And so it worked out. A few days later, on her late afternoon walk she passed the church and saw the vicar by the south door. As she entered the graveyard she momentarily looked away from the church entrance. It was only seconds, yet when she returned her view to the door, the vicar was nowhere to be seen. She rationalised that he had gone inside; however when she reached the door she found it securely locked and the church in darkness. It was at this moment that the young woman became icy cold and unnerved. It suddenly became apparent that there was no clergyman and that she was totally alone in the graveyard. She turned and hurriedly walked back down the church path to the gate, yet as she did so she had the horrible sensation that someone was walking quickly behind her.

When she reached home she turned on all of the cottage's lights and poured herself a stiff drink. She had no doubt that what she had seen and heard was in some way paranormal. Her assumptions were confirmed a few days later when one of the villagers showed her around the sunlit church and related the, supposed ghostly, appearances of the Revd Scott. Of course the villager laughed and scoffed at the idea of ghosts, but the young commercial artist, who kept her experience to herself, was of a different opinion.

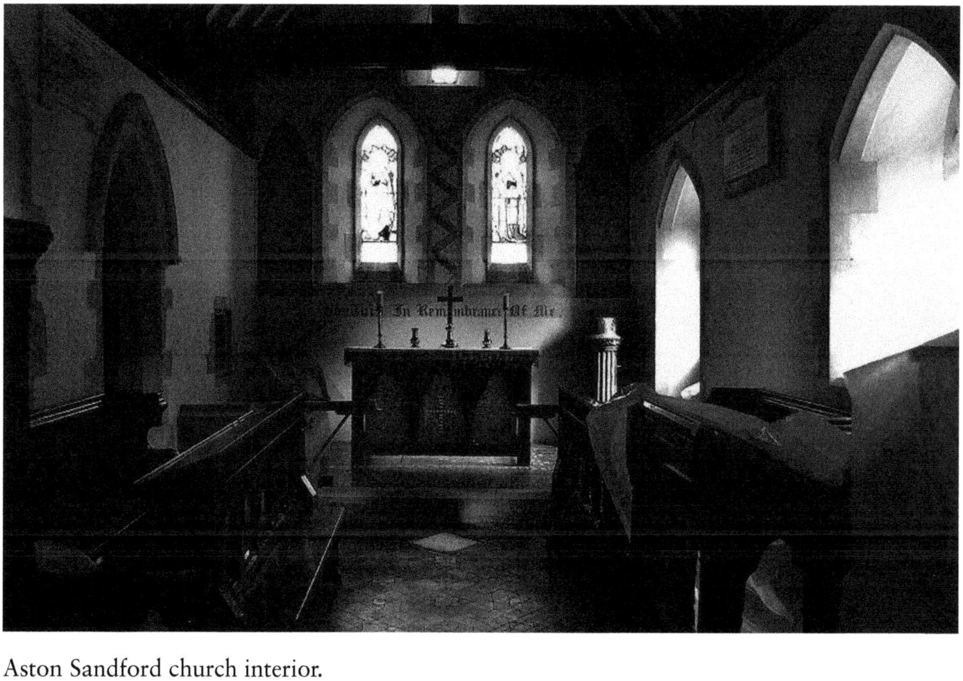

Aston Sandford church interior.

The Ghost of Castle House

Fifteenth-century Castle House in Buckingham is said to be haunted by the ghost of a priest. His apparition has been seen gliding along a corridor which leads to a priest's hole, a place which proved to be his grave. In 1908 the house was being renovated when a small chamber was found hidden beneath the floor of the upper stories directly over the Great Parlour. Within were found the bones of a man along with a crucifix, rosary and the other belongings. It was from the time of the discovery of the corpse that the haunting began.

The clergyman is thought to have been Father Thomas who administered mass and confession to Catherine of Aragon, who had come to Buckingham in the latter part of the 1520s while her husband, King Henry VIII, was seeking grounds for divorce. One day Thomas simply disappeared never to be seen again, until his bones were uncovered in 1908. The great fire of 1725, which swept through Buckingham, destroyed nearly every building in the town except Castle House.

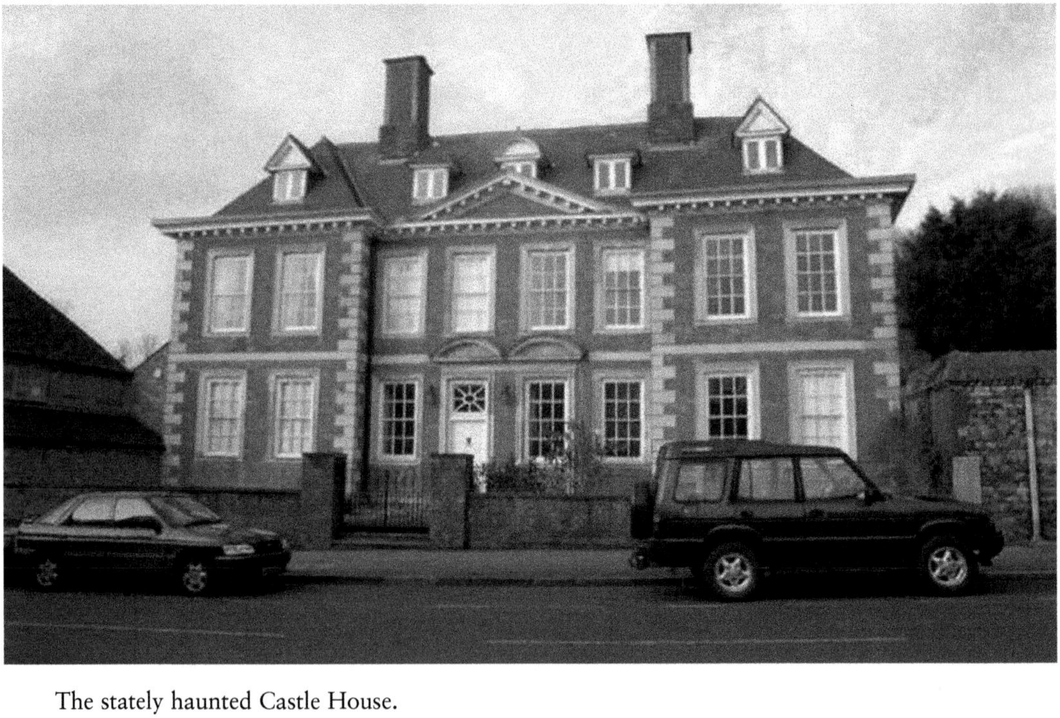

The stately haunted Castle House.

The Child on the Stairs

In 1966, forty-two-year-old Mrs Joan Benson was living with her children in an eighteenth-century house on the outskirts of Buckingham. She had recently separated from her husband, and now had the stressful task of maintaining a home for her family.

Yet, the strain of coping on her own was nothing compared to what would befall her and the seemingly peaceful home she had lived in for three years.

The phenomena commenced unremarkably with the odd unexplainable noise or movement in an upstairs room which was quickly forgotten. Yet, there were also the sounds of footsteps ascending the stairs and sudden slamming of doors which Mrs Benson heard during the day whilst alone in the house, and which were not dismissed so lightly.

However, things soon took a dramatic turn. One Saturday night as she watched TV alone she became aware that the living room had gradually become cold. Without warning she was astonished and shocked to view the form of a young child in a nightgown glide across the room and vanish through a wall. At first Mrs Benson was unsure if she hadn't seen a real child enter and leave such was her amazement.

Shaking her head and not a little unnerved, she fled in to the kitchen, lit a cigarette and wondered if the stress of the estrangement from her husband was beginning to tell. She convinced herself that the vision of the child was a hallucination brought on by tiredness and worry.

However, over the weeks the instances of phenomena gradually increased with the sound of footsteps in the rooms and on the stairs becoming more frequent. Mrs Benson also began to hear soft whispering and indecipherable mutterings throughout the house.

Things took a more disturbing turn when Mrs Benson was awoken on several nights by having her hair pulled, and on occasion her arms pinched. Sitting up in bed she always found the darkened room empty. Curiously, as the phenomena continued, the Benson children seemed to be unaffected by the strange events, and were completely unaware of what their mother was experiencing. We may view this as odd. In most hauntings of this type the focus is invariably a child, or teenager, who unconsciously causes the phenomena, or is affected by it.

One day as Mrs Benson stood at the top of a flight of stairs she had the impression that hands were laid on her shoulders, and that there was a force behind them, as if someone wanted to push her off the landing. Yet, what she describes as most unpleasant was that the feel of the hands were soft and small like those of a child. But it must have been someone, or something which was the same height as herself.

The climax to the haunting culminated in a series of bizarre nightmares which Mrs Benson experienced. In one she says that she had woken in bed and sat up.

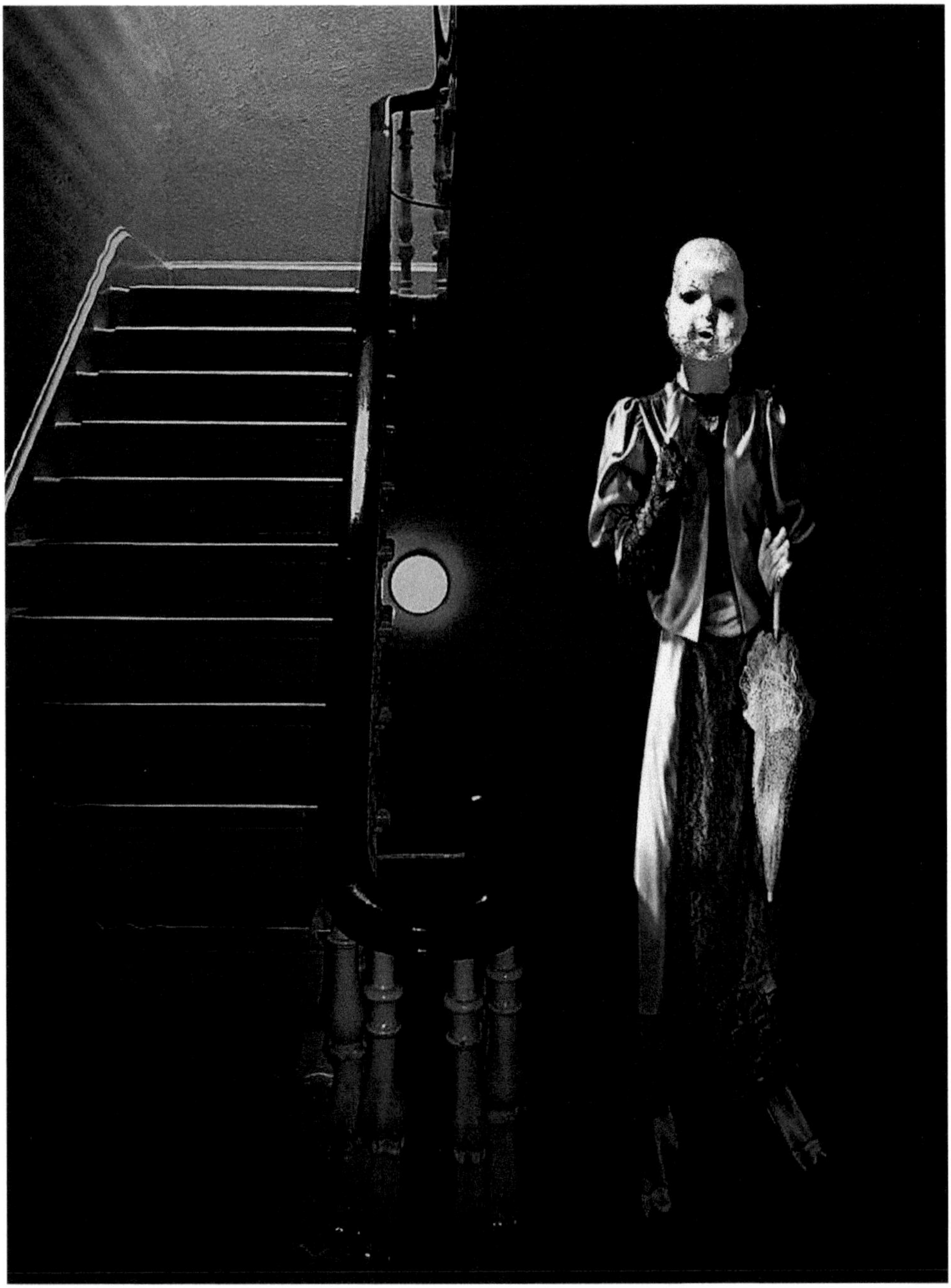

Mrs Benson's terrifying dream.

She could hear soft whisperings outside the room. As she looked across to the bedroom door it ever so gently swung open. Moments later a child's head peeped around the door and looked at her with a most evil expression.

In another nightmare Mrs Benson dreamt she was standing on the top landing of the house at night. She could hear gentle footsteps ascending the stairs. Out of the

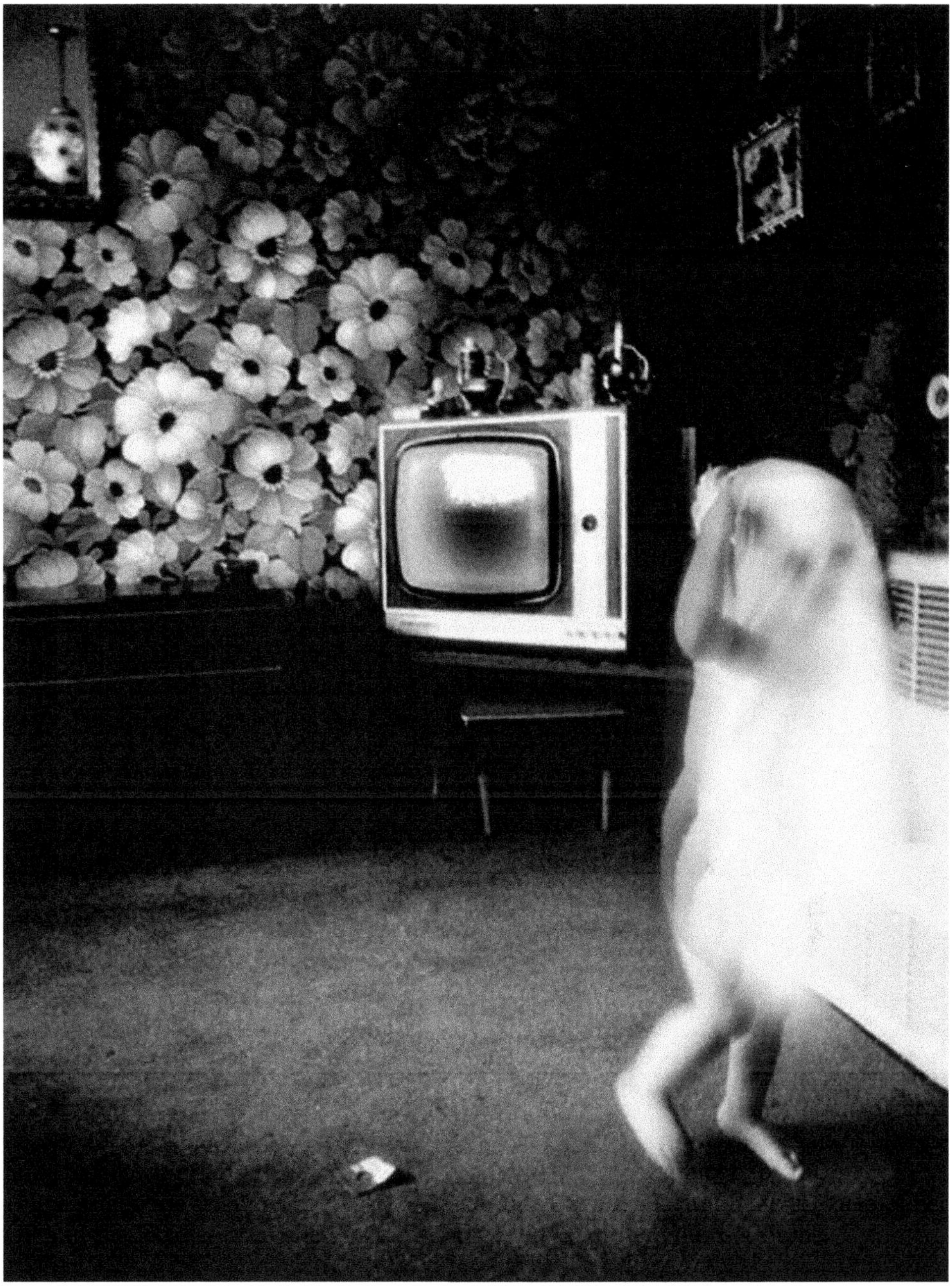

The ghost child which glided across the room.

shadows appeared a child in a nightgown gradually walking up each flight towards her. As the figure started on the final steps Mrs Benson says that it began to change into the grown figure of a woman, but still retained its cherubic, baby face.

Eventually the strain of the disturbances became too much, and with the help of her GP and the local council she and her family were allocated another home.

The Ghost Train

One of the most romantic, and pleasantly eerie, sounds to hear in the dead of night is perhaps the distant whistle of a steam locomotive as it trundles its way through deep cuttings and empty stations en route to remote, unknown towns. I can recall, as a child in 1960s London, laying in bed awake and hearing the far-off hoot, rattle and clack of an express train racing through the night – definitely one of the most evocative and haunting sounds of the small hours.

Yet, the pleasures of a train's distant echo is one thing. To encounter a roaring, clanking goods train which should not be there is a totally different experience. For is it possible for a loco to posses a soul? Can the dismantled steel, iron and brass of forgotten engines return to haunt the tracks they once steamed along. For two unsuspecting young men it is entirely possible.

In November 1983, two barmen who had been working at a public house in High Wycombe were walking home along London Road towards Wycombe marsh. They had reached the junction of Spring Gardens and Pinions Road, and were probably

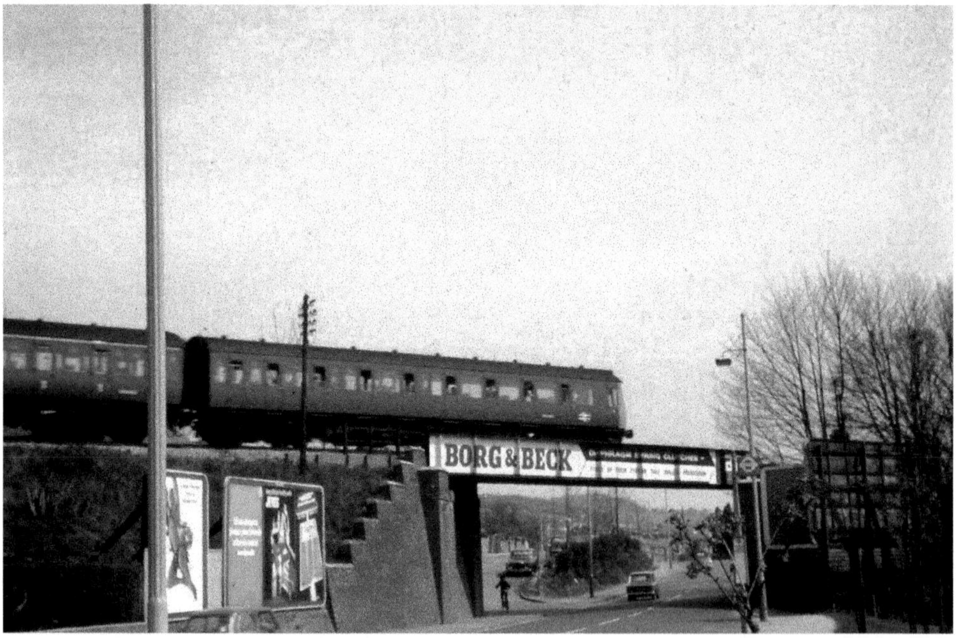

The site of the sounds of a ghost train.

unaware that the raised embankments which rose up on either side of the road once carried the branch railway line from High Wycombe to Maidenhead. The line was closed in the late 1960s and the bridge demolished some years after.

As the men proceeded pass the former railway bridge they heard the approach of a train. Both were surprised, as the time was nearly 3.00 a.m., and it puzzled them that a service would still be running at that hour. Yet, they halted, for they realised that it could not be a train. There was no line. Nonetheless, what they heard was not the clean sound of an electric train or rumble of a diesel, but the unmistakable huff and hiss of a steam locomotive chuffing its way across the bridge.

Both men quickly retraced their steps to get a better look at the embankment, but when they gazed up to where the top of the crossing once was, there was no train to be seen; no belching smoke or glow from its firebox. But still they could hear the sound of the engine. Both stared at each other in astonishment. And then, without warning, the sound ceased. It didn't fade away or become lost in the stillness of the night. One moment they could hear it, the next silence, as if a radio or speaker had been abruptly switched off.

The skeptic would argue that what the men heard could not be a ghost train, for how can the nuts, bolts and metal of a loco and its carriages posses a soul and return to haunt the living. Of course, the skeptic may be right, but then again what we have here is possibly an example of the stone tape. Such a theory suggests that certain actions, be they human, mechanical or perhaps even of a natural nature can sometimes playback their visions and sounds to those who are in the right place at the right time. Science has yet to explain the stone tape recording theory, and until then we will have to contend ourselves with the pleasurable idea that a phantom goods train is still transporting its cargo through High Wycombe to Maidenhead unaware that its body lies in pieces in a forgotten scrapyard.

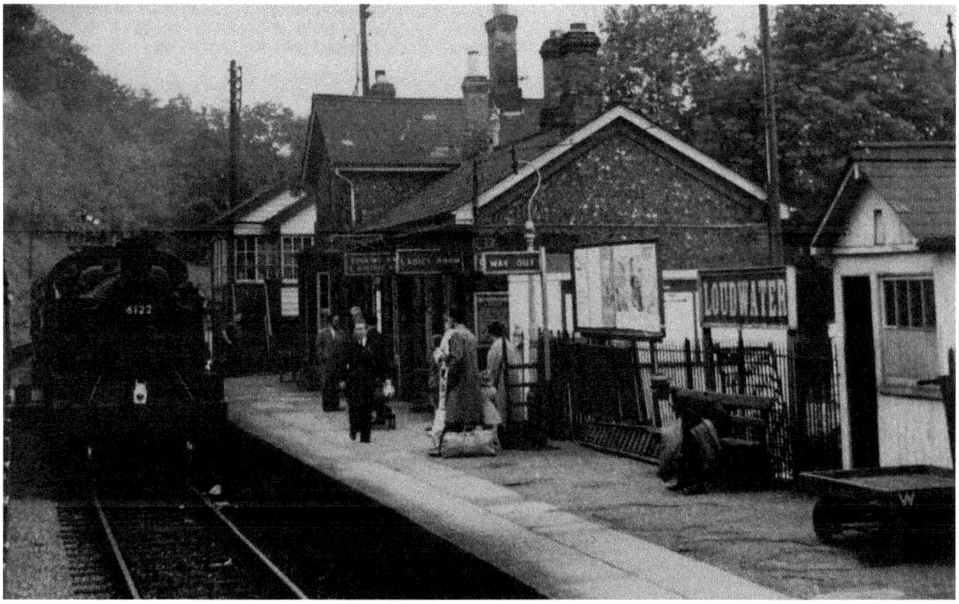

Does the ghost train still makes its way through High Wycombe?

The Angel at the Bus Stop

One of the misconceptions about the paranormal is that it is in some way malevolent. Apart from extremely rare instances of poltergeist phenomena in which people have suffered minor injuries, no ghost, in the history of ghosts, ever harmed those who have encountered them. Of course, the fear and alarm of experiencing something which is unknown and disturbing can leave the percipient in a state of shock. Yet, in many cases the opposite can occur, and even bring about a feeling of benevolence and happiness.

On Christmas Eve in that harsh winter of 1963, twenty-year-old Stan Mathias was invited to a friend's party in Beaconsfield new town. The prospect of an enjoyable evening seemed promising, and the young man travelled the considerable distance from Gerrards Cross to attend. And so it proved, for he did not leave the party until 2.00 a.m. on Christmas Day morning.

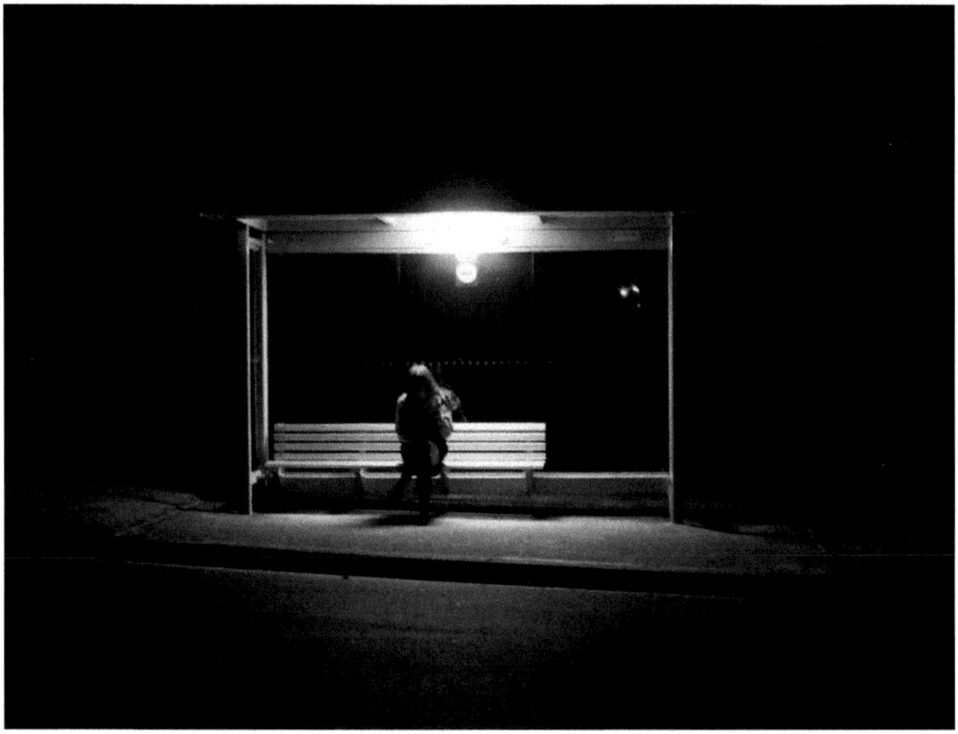

Can bus stops be haunted?

On leaving his friend's house he planned to walk along the road which runs from the new town and on to the old town, and then on to the A 40 to Gerrards Cross . So it was that Stan found himself striding homeward along empty, Christmas, lamp-lit streets. However, the young man did come across another person that night, a strange encounter he recalls today with crisp clarity.

Some way along the route to the old town he noticed a woman standing alone at a bus stop. Dressed in a white mackintosh, her blond hair and smiling face seemed to Stan to radiate a warm, benevolent glow. She appeared to be staring back down the road as if looking for an oncoming bus, and completely unaware of Stan. Somewhat surprised that the lady should be unaccompanied at that hour, he passed her and continued on his way. It did occur to him to inform her that there was no bus service, it being Christmas Day, but thought better of it lest she took it as a cheap chat-up line.

He reached the high street of Beaconsfield old town and was soon at the junction with the A40. Yet, much to his utter surprise, at a bus stop stood the same woman he had seen some fifteen minutes earlier. This seemed impossible. He would have certainly noticed if she had overtaken him, and no car had passed in which she might have been offered a lift.

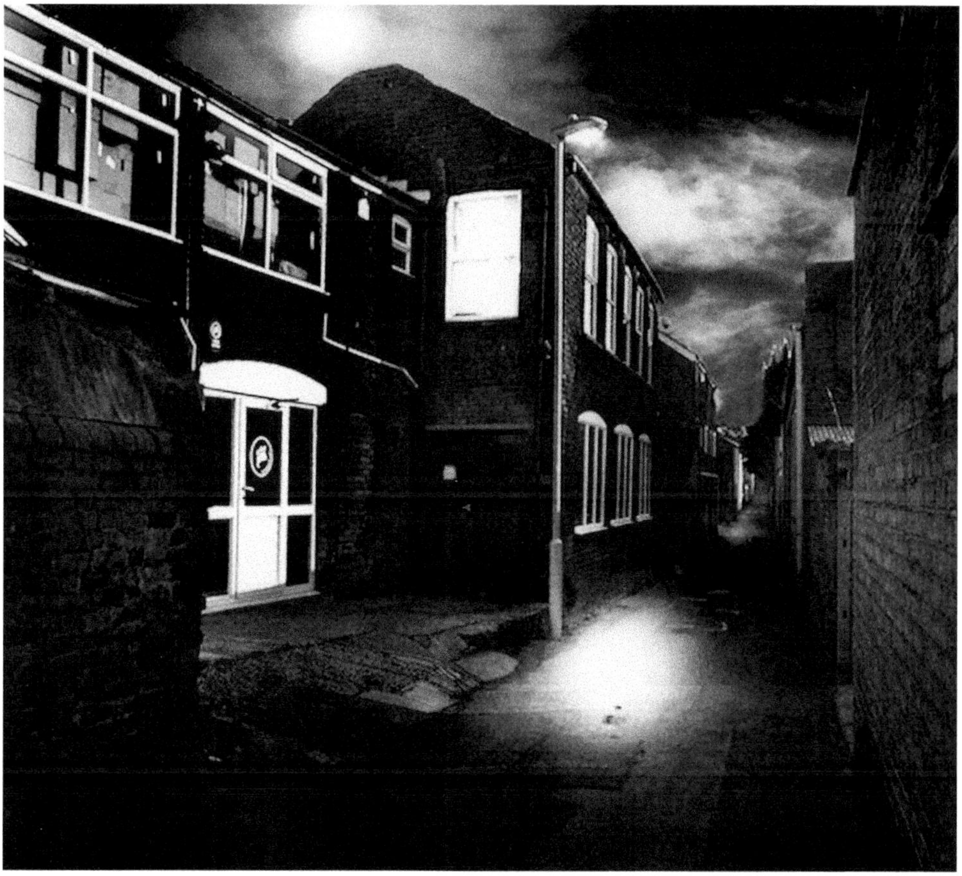

Stan Mathias made his long way home through deserted streets.

As he looked, he noticed that she once again stared back down the road as if expecting someone to arrive, and appeared to be completely unaware of his presence. As the young man proceeded on his way, he continued to glance back over his shoulder to see if the woman was still there, which she was. It was when Stan had covered some distance from the bus stop that he once more turned to look back, but the woman was nowhere to be seen. No bus or car had appeared that she might have boarded, and she would have still been in sight had she chosen to walk in the opposite direction. Stan stopped and looked back bewildered. The woman had gone.

Even though the appearance of the woman, and her subsequent vanishing, seemed uncanny, Stan recalls that he felt no threat or fear from his encounter. On the contrary, he says that an overwhelming feeling of happiness came over him, and as he walked he started singing one of his favourite songs. The next thing he knew he had reached his home in Gerrards Cross, and was opening his front door. Yet, he had no recollection of traversing the tiring 6-mile distance. His long trek seemed to be have been completed in a moment's blissful haze, as if he was carried home by some benign energy, and the thought of the miserable miles erased from his mind.

Stan is convinced that the mystery woman at the bus stop played some caring part in his journey back home. Was she a ghost, or a benevolent spirit which helps the weary traveller home? For Stan, he prefers to think of her as an angel – his Christmas angel at the bus stop.

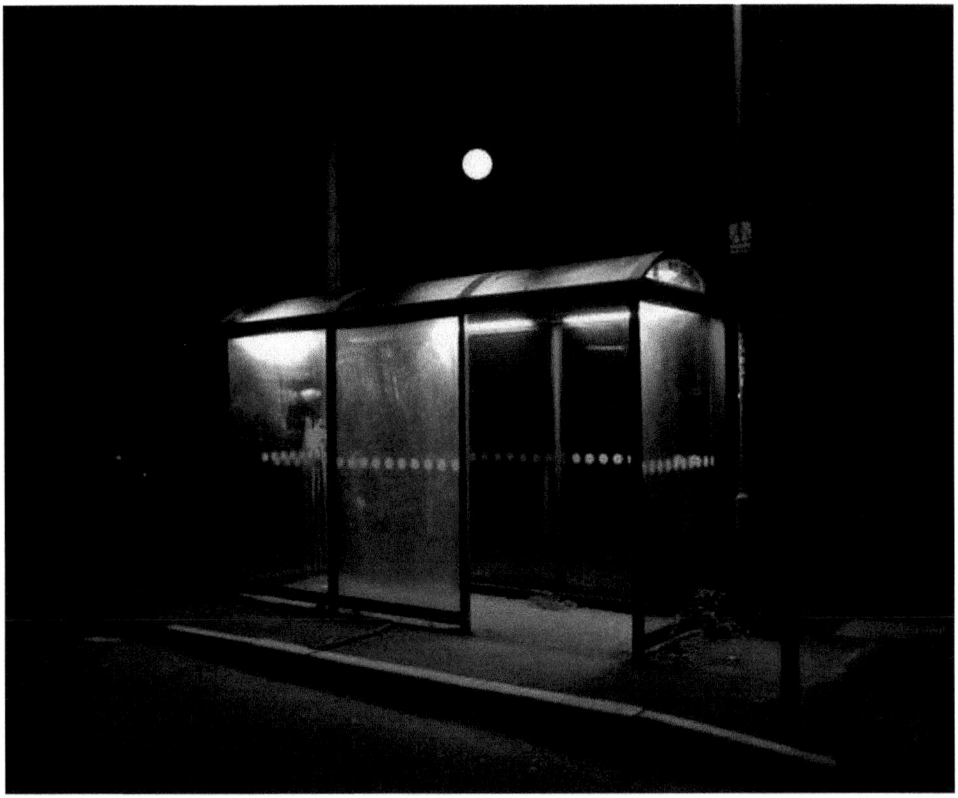

Bus stops – islands of sanctuary in the sea of darkness.

The Smiling Highwayman

One of the most frustrating facts about paranormal research is that we rarely see a ghost when we are consciously looking for one. Also, we have the puzzle as how and why the paranormal works, and why ghosts choose to make their presence known to us. Even if it's the apparition of a smiling highwayman in the middle of bustling Milton Keynes.

In 1999, Shirley was living with her partner and daughter, together with her daughter's baby, on a housing estate close to the town's centre. One night she went into the kitchen to get a glass of water. She did not need to turn on the kitchen light because of the illumination from the estate's precinct street lamps. As she filled her glass, she nonchalantly looked from the kitchen window. To her surprise she saw a young man leaning against a tree and looking back at her. He was perhaps in his early twenties and dressed in the fashion of an eighteenth-century highwayman. His long, dark, curly hair hung down over his shoulders, and a frockcoat, frilly shirt, cravat, breeches and knee-length riding boots completed the attire.

As he looked at the astonished mother, a broad smile played across his face. For a few moments Shirley stared in amazement before calling for her daughter. In the time it took to look away and gain her daughter's attention, the young man had gone. It seemed as if he had simply vanished into thin air.

The puzzle of the smiling highwayman played on Shirley's nerves for the rest of the night. He was no doubt a late-night reveller from a fancy dress party who had had too much to drink. However, events were soon to take on a more disturbing tone for the family.

Some days later, Shirley's daughter's boyfriend came to spend the night. During the small hours he needed to visit the toilet. Returning to the bedroom, he looked across at what he thought was his girlfriend asleep in bed, but it wasn't her. The whole flat was awakened by the boyfriend's screams. It took a few minutes for the terrified man to calm down and collect himself, yet what he related brought a disbelieving shiver to all present. He had entered the bedroom and made to get back into bed, yet as he looked down on his girlfriend he could see it wasn't her face; it was the face of a long-haired young man who smiled back at him.

It wasn't long after this incident that the vision of the smiling man was once again seen. One night, as Shirley and her partner slept, she was awoken by the sound of his labored breathing as he gasped for air. He was experiencing a sleep apnoea attack, and she hurriedly grabbed hold of his shoulders and began to shake him, shouting 'wake up, wake up and breathe'. Coughing and spluttering, he quickly gained consciousness, yet on waking looked at Shirley with almost wide eyed disbelief.

'What is it?' She hastily asked him. 'It wasn't you shaking me,' he replied. 'It was a young man with long hair.'

The smiling man was not again seen in the flat or outside the kitchen window. Yet, that was not the end of the story. One night as Shirley and her daughter were returning from the supermarket they passed a young man who they noticed was dressed very unusually. He was clad in clothing from the eighteenth century. As the young man passed, both mother and daughter stopped and looked at one another with open mouths and furrowed brows. Yet, on turning to take a second look at the strangely dressed person, there was no one in sight.

Shirley never again experienced anything strange in her home, but she is philosophical about what she saw that night. She says that it never really troubled her, for she finds the idea of an afterlife absolutely fascinating. She never found out who the ghostly young man was. She likes to think that it was a benign spirit protecting her family.

Shirley has since moved on from Milton Keynes and, as far is known, her former home has been free of any further paranormal activity. If what she saw was indeed a ghost, is it possible that a future tenant, who gazes form their kitchen window in the small hours, will again see a smiling, benign highwayman staring back?

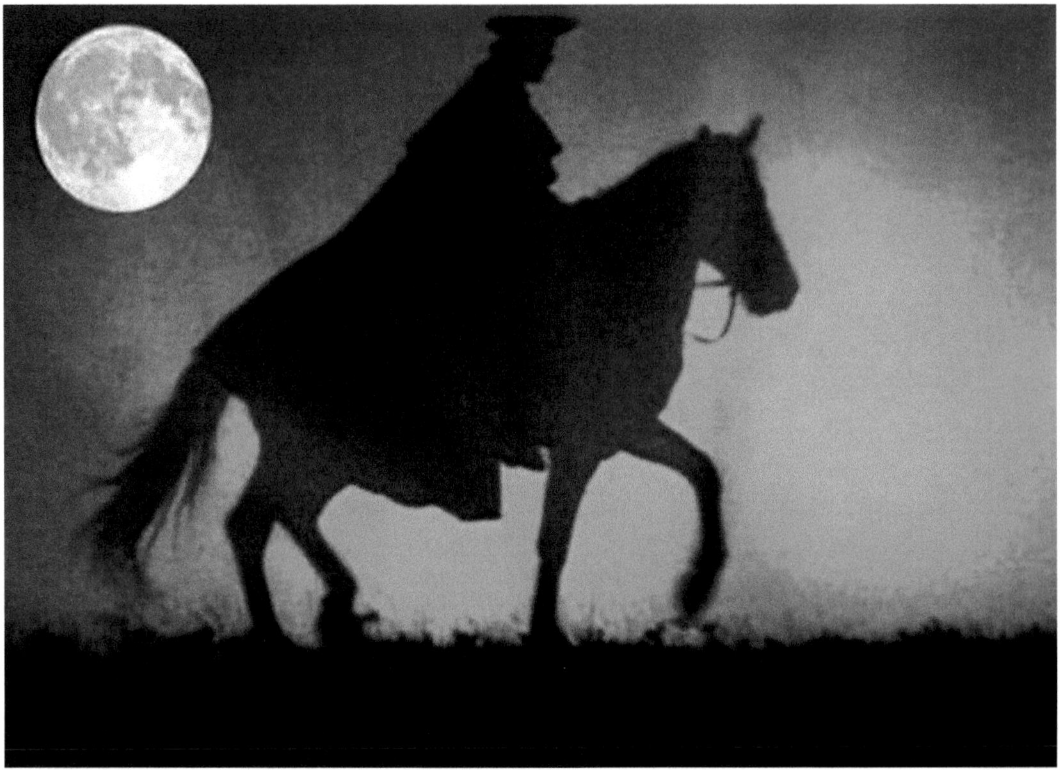

The smiling Cavalier.

The Grinning Man

In June 1975, Susan Bradshaw came to live and work as a barmaid at the Bell House Hotel near Gerrards Cross. Her first few months in residence were busy, yet relatively uneventful. However, one night, some months later, that was to change.

As Kay relaxed in the bath after a tiring day, she was suddenly shaken from her warm, foaming slumber by the bathroom being plunged into darkness. Thinking there had been a power cut, she leapt out of the tub and opened the bathroom door. However, the rest of the building's lights were on. Puzzled, she looked about the room and saw that the bulb lay on the wet floor. It had inexplicably come loose from its socket and fallen noiselessly to the linoleum. What was even more mystifying was that the bulb was still warm. Its brittleness should have shattered on impact. Kay reasoned there had to be a rational explanation and put the episode to the back of her mind.

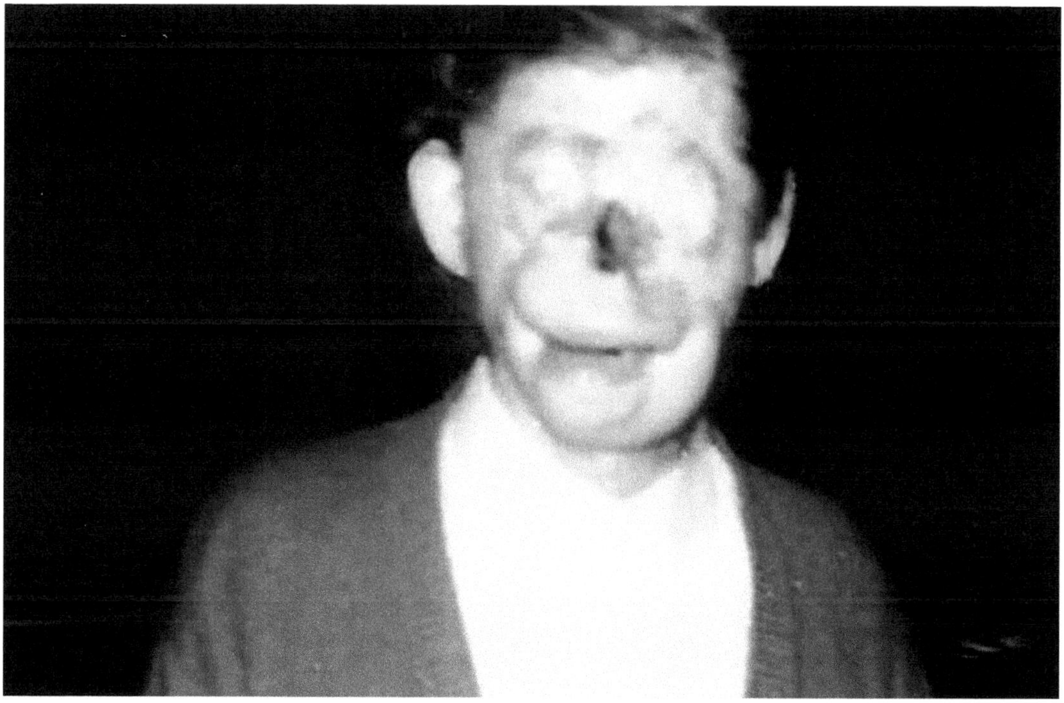

The grinning man.

A few weeks later another curious incident occurred, this time with a more sinister aspect. Stepping into the bathroom one night, Kay reached for the string pull of the light switch. But as she did so the cord suddenly seemed to swish up and wrap itself around her neck in a violent whiplash movement. The light came on and she could see that the cord had twisted itself tightly around her throat. Grabbing the cord, she untangled it from her neck and backed out of the bathroom in shock. It seemed that the cord had intentionally whipped up towards her, yet that had to be preposterous. Once again she put the incident down to a unexplainable fluke. Nonetheless, the new barmaid was soon to experience another inexplicable, yet far more terrifying incident.

Some weeks later she was awoken in the small hours by the sound of rustling in her bedroom. Sitting up in bed, she looked across to the door and could see the polythene covering of a recently dry-cleaned dress rippling and billowing as if a breeze was playing against it. But the night was hot and still, with not a breath of wind.

After a few minutes the sounds ceased and Susan went to lay back down. As she did so she turned and saw a figure standing next to the bed, the person bent menacingly over her, grinning and squinting as he pushed his face ever so closer. She at once leapt screaming from the bed and ran out of the room. Her colleagues found her in great distress, and immediately searched the room, but it was empty. Despite reassurances from her friends that it must have been a dream, Susan refused to sleep another night there.

The young barmaid's weird experiences were soon discussed by people in the pub. One day an elderly customer asked her if she had heard of the Chinese man who hanged himself in the top room. His gambling and drinking had forced his wife to leave him, and he sank into a desperate melancholy. One hot night, with all hope gone, he hung himself from a wardrobe by the bedroom door – the wardrobe by the bedroom door in Susan's room.

The Amorous Hitch-hiker

Many accounts of paranormal phenomena are sometimes so fantastic and disturbing that one wonders if the stories have come straight from the pen of a Hollywood screenplay writer, for they contain the two essential ingredients for modern-day cinema: sex and horror.

Some years ago, on an uncertain date, a young man was travelling home to Winslow on the main Buckingham to Aylesbury road. He was returning in a foul mood because of a date with a young lady which hadn't gone very well. They had argued and he stormed off.

It was late, and as the man drove along the deserted road he saw a beautiful woman by the side of the carriageway who seemed to be hitch-hiking. He stopped and offered her a lift.

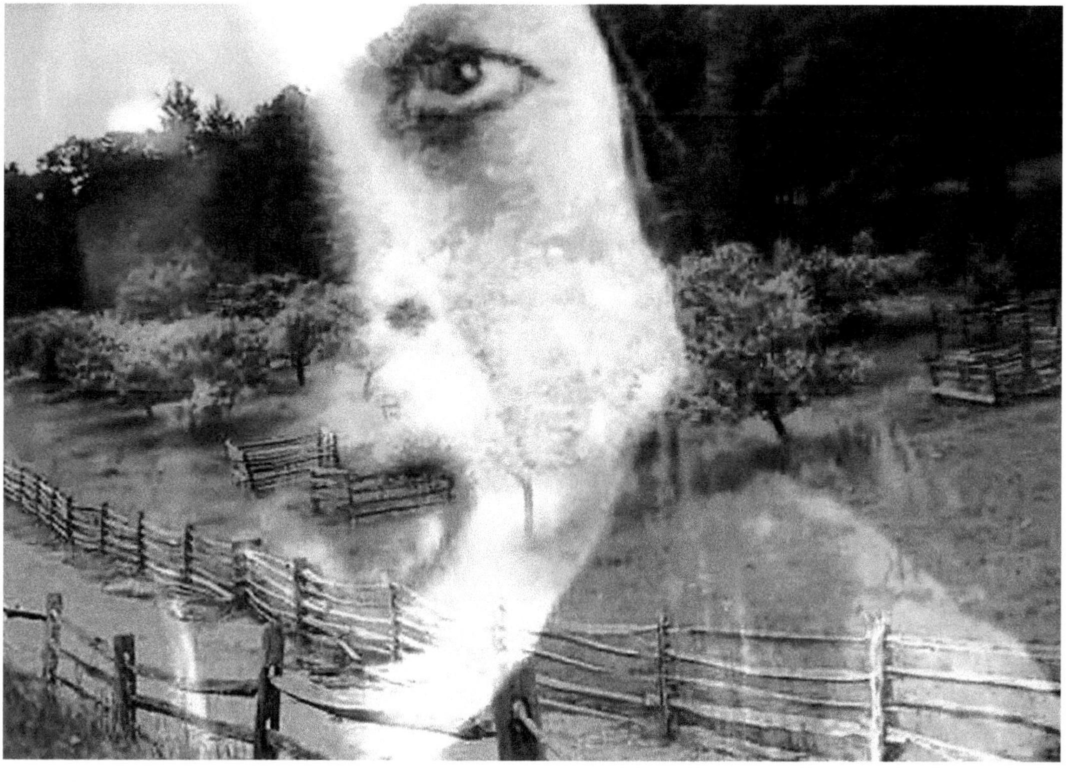

The amorous hitch-hiker.

As the woman sat next to the driver she began to fondle him. He pulled the car over and took the mysterious woman into a public toilet. It was there that the two indulged in sex of a most 'intimate' nature. Following this they left the toilet and returned to the car and continued ravishing each other.

It was then that the young man began to experience what he describes as a nightmare. He became aware of a strange smell, something like burning. He thought it was a discarded cigarette. He began to choke, and thought he would pass out.

As he looked at the woman a horrifying change came over her. Her features were altering. The young man looked on terrified. No longer was there a beautiful woman, but some haggard, disgusting old crone with a disfigured face. The man pushed her back with all the force he could muster, but the old hag just looked down on him and laughed. Eventually as the man screamed and screamed, the woman vanished.

Although disturbed by his experience, he was reluctant to share it with friends or family. In time he related his ordeal to a local paranormal investigator who listened with interest.

Over the years two other men had come forward with similar experiences, yet they too had remained silent over their encounter. Not, it would seem, that they feared ridicule for saying they had seen a ghost, but rather that they had indulged in sex with a old hag in a public toilet.

Such accounts as these inevitably make us ask if the people who experience them are in some way dreaming or possibly under the influence of drugs. All I can say is that as a paranormal investigator all strange phenomena, however bizarre, must be recorded. If they are hoaxes, so be it – even fraudulent accounts must be taken into consideration if we are to sort the wheat from the chaff and establish a basis for fact. On the other hand if subsequent people come forward who report the same experience, then we must reconsider all possibilities.

The Woman in Black

Those readers who often drive through Loudwater and negotiate the roundabout for either Tescos superstore, the M40 or straight on to Holtspur and Beaconsfield may be unaware that behind the trees adjacent to the junction stands a grand Victorian mansion which has a curious past.

Burleighfield House is a substantial twenty-room residence set in 3 acres of grounds which back onto open countryside. It was built in 1860 by Thomas Burch Ford, a wealthy Loudwater Mill owner.

Following Burch Ford's death, the house became in turn the home of a leather goods manufacturer, a guest house and a private school. In 1960 Burleighfield achieved a moderate level of fame when it became the home of master stained-glass designer Patrick Reyntiens. He established the Burleighfield Arts school and studios. It was Reyntiens who designed the stained glass for Liverpool Cathedral, Christ Church, Oxford, and the baptistery at Coventry Cathedral.

By 2003 the studios had run into financial difficulties and were put into liquidation. The house remained unoccupied until 2005 when it was taken over by a Yellow Pages publisher. Given such an interesting past it is no wonder that Burleighfield is said to be home to the ghost of a mysterious woman in black.

On a bright Sunday morning in September 2005 a workman arrived at Burleighfield House to clean the windows. The building was locked and empty for the weekend. Placing his ladder up at one of the first-floor rooms he commenced cleaning. Without warning he saw the figure of a woman dressed in black Victorian clothes descend the stairs. She had a most horrible, deathly pallor to her face, and seemed not so much to walk as glide. The shock nearly made him lose his grip on the ladder and fall.

The window cleaner was not the only one to experience the woman in black. Staff and workmen have reported seeing and feeling her ghost, and the upper rooms and corridors of the house are thought to be where she lurks to terrify any unsuspecting sceptics.

This author has a special fondness for Burleighfield as, before becoming a writer, and between 2005 and 2010, I was employed there as a caretaker. A grand Victorian mansion set in pleasant, landscaped grounds was a lovely place to work until I discovered that the house had another, sinister aspect – a ghostly, evil-looking woman in black who walked the house and the grounds. On several dark winter mornings I would walk alone up the driveway to the darkened house to open up and commence work. I made my way through the rooms, along the shadowy corridors and up the stairs always with trepidation. Would the woman in black leap out on me? I was glad when the staff arrived and I had company. Even ghost hunters get anxious.

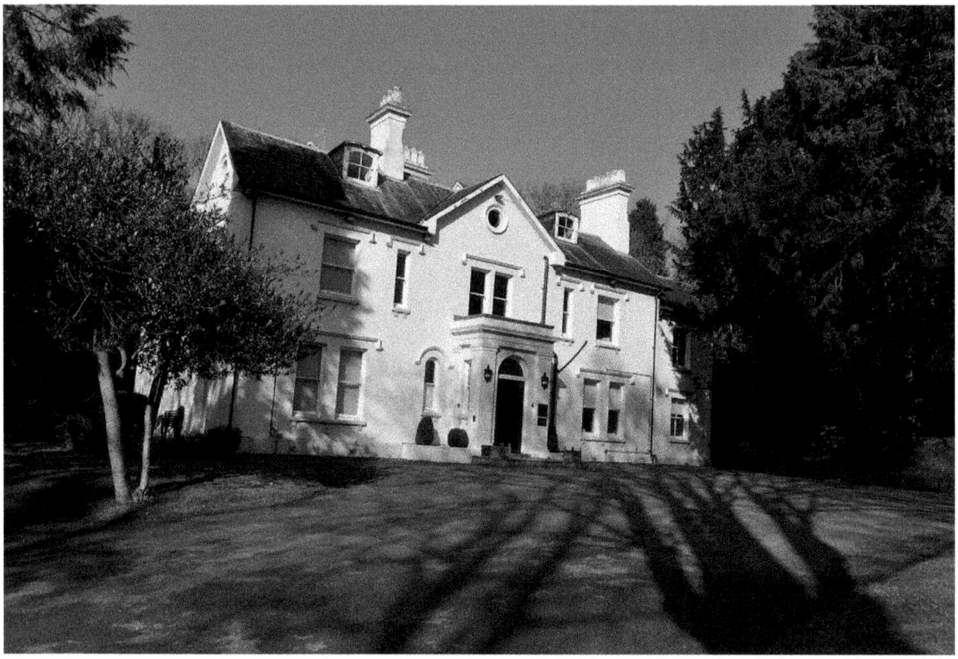

Haunted Burleighfield House.

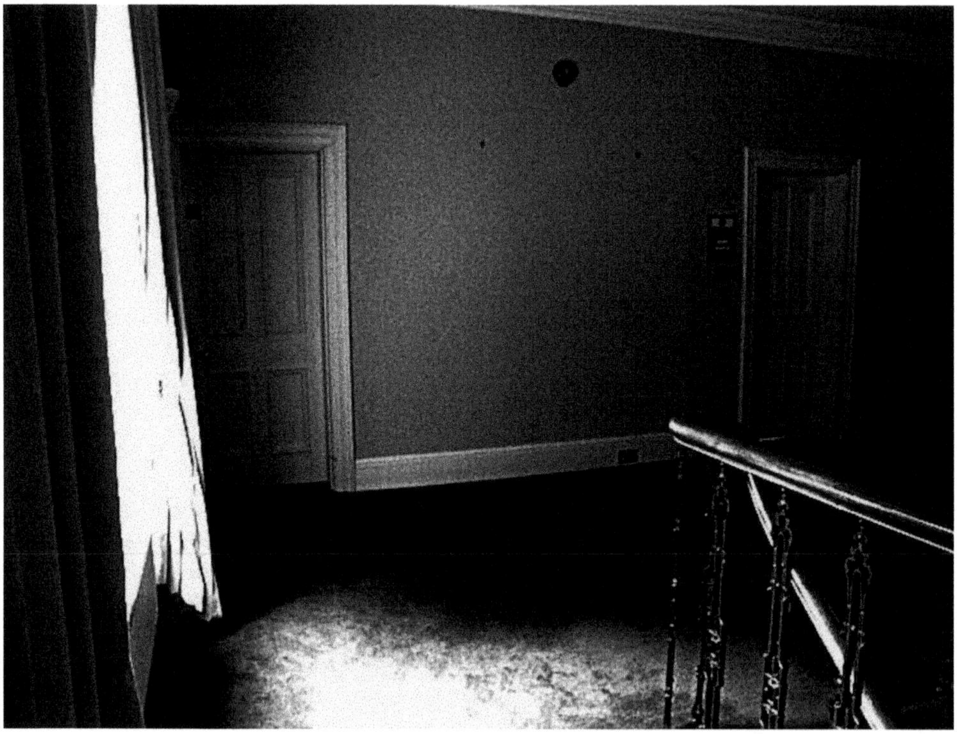

Burleighfield interior.

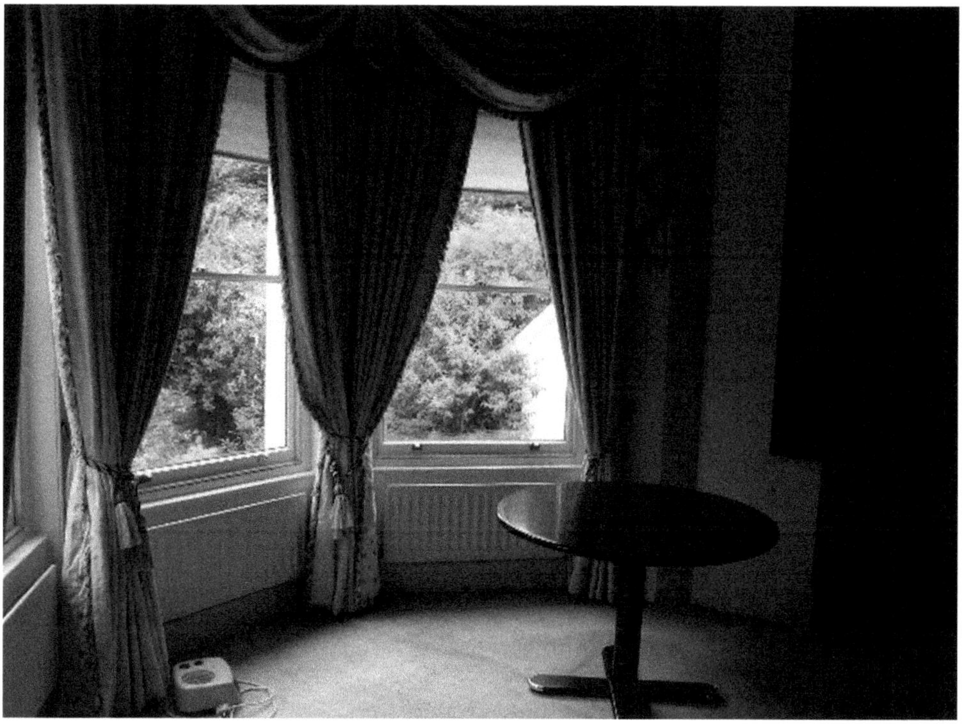

Haunted bedroom at Burleighfield.

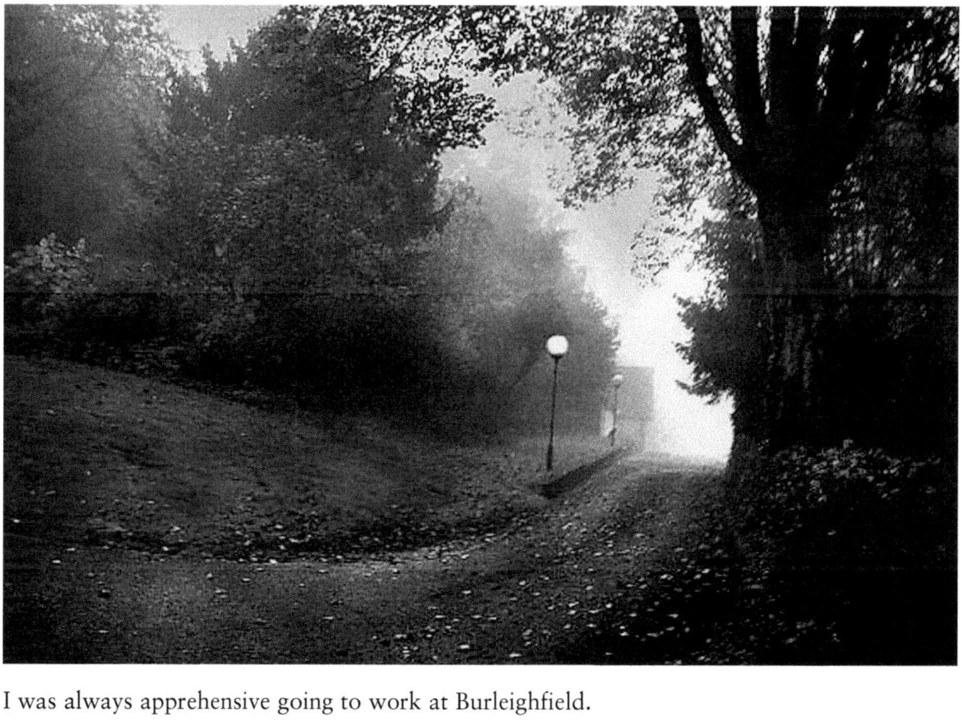

I was always apprehensive going to work at Burleighfield.

'There's a Man in the Road'

On an unspecified date in the 1860s or 1870s, a coach en route from London to Oxford stopped at Beaconsfield to take on a fresh team of horses. It was late, and the driver was eager to make for High Wycombe before dark. The evening was misty and the coach, on leaving the town, was soon lost within the increasing mirk. The road from Beaconsfield to Holtspur, at that time a remote farmstead, is fairly level. Beyond the farmstead the route begins a long, gradual descent to Loudwater, which allowed the driver to pick up speed, thundering the fresh horses down White Hill (the present A40). At the foot of the hill, by Wooburn Moor, the road makes a slight dip (adjacent to today's Tescos superstore car park). As the coach came hurtling down into the impenetrable fog the horses panicked and the driver lost control, crashing the vehicle into the icy waters of a local pond. All on board, including the horses, perished. It is said that on the anniversary of the tragedy the cries and screams of the doomed passengers and neighing horses can be heard echoing throughout the area.

Some seventy years later on a misty winter's night in 1936 a lorry was travelling down White Hill towards Wycombe. As it reached Wooburn Moor a man dressed in a black coat suddenly stepped from the side of the road and into the path of the truck; it was too late to stop. Both the driver and his mate watched in horror as they saw the figure go under the vehicle. Convinced they had struck the man, they hastened from their cab to lend assistance, but when they went to look for the body there was nothing to be found. The road was empty. Even so, the distraught men informed the local police who also could find no trace of the man. Later, the officer who had attended to the scene informed the shaken driver that other people had reported the same thing happening to them on that stretch of road. Could the apparition of the man in black be the spirit of one of the ill-fated passengers from the doomed coach? Who can say? It would certainly add substance to the story of the fatal crash.

I was to later learn that the two men, although shaken by their experience, carried on their journey, which would have taken many more hours as they were delivering their cargo to the city of Gloucester. They proceeded on the route through Wycombe and out of the town by way of the A40 and on to West Wycombe. They quickly passed through the sleeping village and onward towards Stokenchurch. However, just as they were leaving West Wycombe their lorry started to experience engine trouble. Coughing, sputtering and losing power, it gradually slowed until it was barely moving. Back in 1936, and at that hour, the prospect of meeting other traffic on the road was remote. However, as the lorry began to crawl to a halt the driver and his mate looked ahead and were surprised to see the red tail lights of a large vehicle stationary in the middle of the road. Soon they could see the frantic waving of a man with a flashlight who seemed to be signalling for them to stop.

The lorry finally coughed its last immediately behind the stationary vehicle and was approached by the waiving man.

'Hello pal, the man said, you couldn't't give us a hand, I've broken down?'

The driver and his mate looked at the dead dashboard of their own vehicle and told the other driver it wasn't their night; they were having trouble as well. Both lorry crews were soon looking under the bonnets of the respective trucks trying to see what was wrong. Presently cigarettes were passed around and small talk struck up.

'Its been an odd old journey', said the first truck driver, who had waved the flashlight. 'About an hour ago we were just outside Wycombe coming down White Hill and me and my mate could have sworn we hit some chap standing in the middle of the road. Walked right out in front of the lorry. I tried to brake but it was too late. Fair shook us up it did. Strange thing is, when we went to see if he was ok, there wasn't a sign of him. He was nowhere to be seen.'

Both driver and mate looked at each other with open mouths and raised brows. The two crews then exchanged experiences and all agreed it was indeed a peculiar coincidence. Soon after, without finding a reason for the engine fault of both trucks, the two lorries' ignitions were turned and, much to everyone's surprise, started without trouble. It was indeed turning into an unusual night.

With everything seemingly back to normal the trucks moved off and carried on their respective journeys. The first lorry had only a short distance to travel before it unloaded its cargo and returned to London. Toots were exchanged as the trucks went their separate ways and their red tail lights disappeared in to the night. About an hour later the crew had delivered their load and were now making the return trip down the A40 between Stokenchurch and West Wycombe. Just before they were to enter the village they saw up ahead the lights of a vehicle stationary by the side of the road. The lights were flashed indicating they wanted the approaching truck to stop. As the lorry slowed and neared, they could see a man in the road gesticulating for the vehicle to pull over. They drew alongside and heard the man say he had broken down. The driver and his mate looked at each other and shook their heads.

'You just come through Wycombe?', they asked.

'Yeah', came the reply. 'Nearly ran over some chap standing in the road at the bottom of White Hill. When we went to look, he wasn't there.'

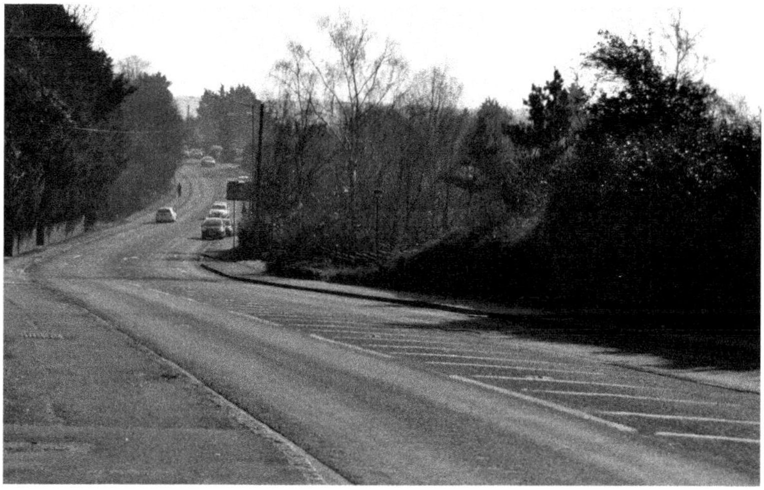

Site of the man in the road.

The Babes in the Wood

On an October night in 1995, fifty-four-year-old Michael Powell, a keen treasure hunter, went to the village of Penn, just outside High Wycombe, eager to explore the adjacent fields for ancient artefacts such as coins, buttons and broaches dropped and lost over the centuries by long-gone residents of the village. Past expeditions at other sites during daylight, however, had seen him flee the wrath of farmers outraged that their crops were being trampled and crushed by hooligan treasure hunters. Consequently, Powell decided to carry out his metal-detecting activities under cover of darkness. Parking his car in a lay-by partway along Common Wood Lane he made his way on foot up through Pugh's Wood and out into the fields near To Puttenham Place Farm, and on to the very path where Sara Osborne had encountered the strange figure of the headless man eight years earlier. On this night Powell would also come into contact with something equally uncanny, and no less disturbing.

Listening for the bleep on his metal detector and keeping an eye out for vigilant landowners he silently explored the fields, yet after an hour of fruitless searching he decided that there was little, if anything, of worth to be unearthed. He decided to pack up and return home.

He made his way back in to Pugh's Wood and down to his car. He had only gone so far into the trees when he heard voices. He stopped and listened intently, and realised that they were the laughs and shouts of children. He was puzzled. What were children doing in a wood at that hour? As he continued to listen, the voices seemed to be coming closer. It struck him that because it was 3.00 a.m., the children had to be accompanied by an adult, and if he himself were discovered, he would be in the embarrassing situation of explaining his own presence at that hour. He remained still and continued to listen. He was relieved to hear the voices of the children heading away from him. Yet, just as he thought they had moved off to the far side of the wood, he once again heard them, but this time they were from his rear. He quickly spun around. The laughter and singing of the children was rapidly heading in his direction, but there was no sound of the snapping of twigs or the rustle of bushes, only the playful yelps and shouts of two youngsters.

As the sounds came closer, Powell expected the children to appear, but there was nothing to be seen in the darkness of the wood. Just as quickly as the voices had sounded behind him they immediately changed course and now emanated from the direction of the fields, seemingly fading and then sounding close again. Powell swung left, right and behind wondering what was happening. The sound of the children seemed to be all around him. It was at this point that he became scared and immediately realised that what he was hearing was abnormal. Hurriedly, he moved down through the wood and back to his car. He got in and, before starting the engine, wound the window down and listened. There were no sounds coming from the wood, only the wind in the trees. He quickly drove away shaking his head, his eyes on the illuminated road, expecting at any moment to see two ghostly children walk out in front of him.

Michael Powell, who died in 2005, was a friend of the author of this book, and the above encounter was related over a pint in a Wycombe pub not long after the episode. Powell knew of my interest in ghosts and, convinced he had indeed heard the spirits of two children, asked if I could throw any light on his experience. At the time I couldn't. It appeared to be a one-off incident, and one I had never before come across. If the phantom children had been experienced by others, then they had kept their silence.

Powell never returned to the wood either by day or night, but for many years was intrigued and baffled by what he had heard that night. The detectorist, in his search for ancient relics, had explored many locations during the small hours and often in places many of us would hesitate to venture after dark. But he took this all in his stride, and was not a person to become easily spooked by being alone in a field or wood at night. This experience in Pugh's Wood had been the only time in his detecting career when he felt truly frightened.

The puzzle of the phantom children would have remained a mystery had not a chance browse on the internet some years later revealed a distressing, yet intriguing coda to the story.

On 19 November 1941, six-year-old Kathleen Trendle and Doreen Hearne, aged eight, were on their way home from Tylers Green School in Penn. They had reached

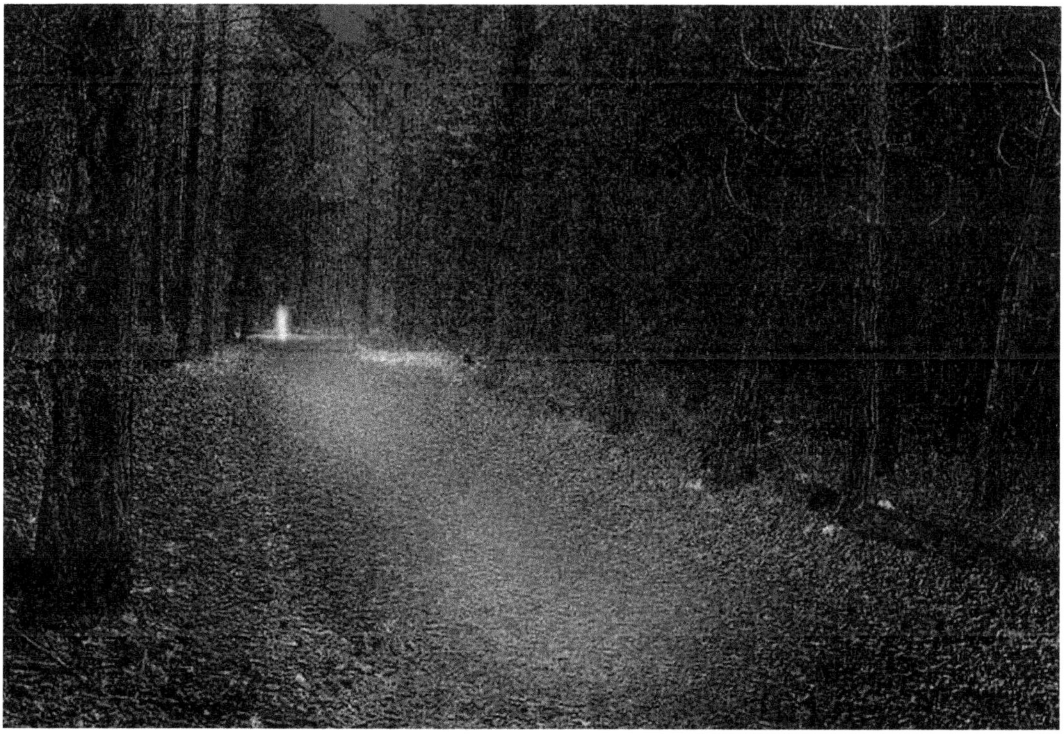

Do ghost children still haunt the woods around Tylers Green and Penn?

the crossroads by Elm Road and Common Wood Lane which runs alongside Pugh's Wood when an army truck pulled up beside them. The driver leaned out of his cab and offered the two girls a ride. Both got in, and the truck drove off in the direction of the village of Penn Street. The children did not return home that night, and three days later their bodies were discovered in a nearby wood. Both had been strangled and stabbed.

Close by were the tyre tracks of a lorry and a large patch of oil. There was also Doreen's gas mask holder and a khaki handkerchief with the laundry mark RA1019. A twelve-year-old boy had told police that he saw the two girls getting into the truck, and gave the unit identification marks of the lorry. The vehicle was quickly traced to a unit, 341 Battery, 86 Field Regiment, Royal Artillery, in Yoxford, Suffolk, and they soon came across the truck with a leaking back axle. The tyre tracks matched the impressions taken from the scene. The driver was twenty-six-year-old gunner Harold Hill. He had the laundry mark RA1019 and his fingerprints were found to match those on the discarded gas mask container. When his kit was examined his spare uniform was found to have bloodstains on it. His plea of insanity was rejected and he was hanged at Oxford Castle on 1 May 1942.

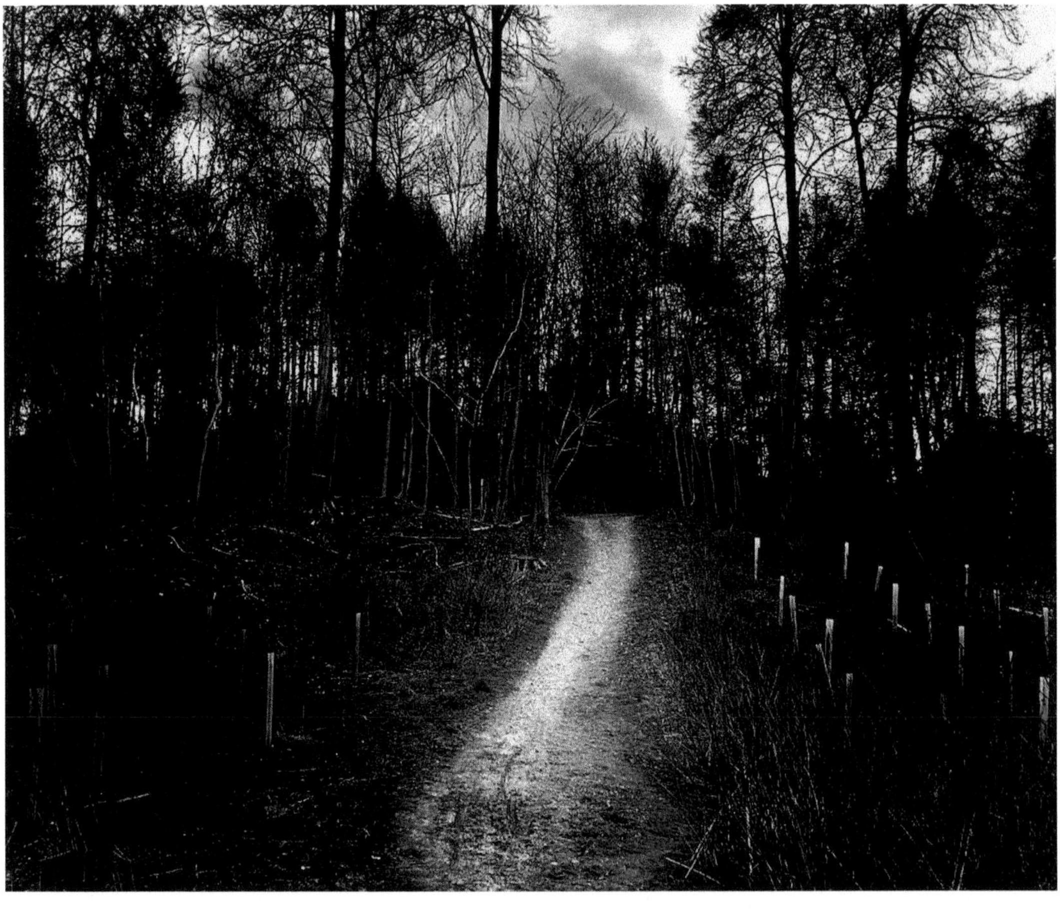

Eerie Common Wood.

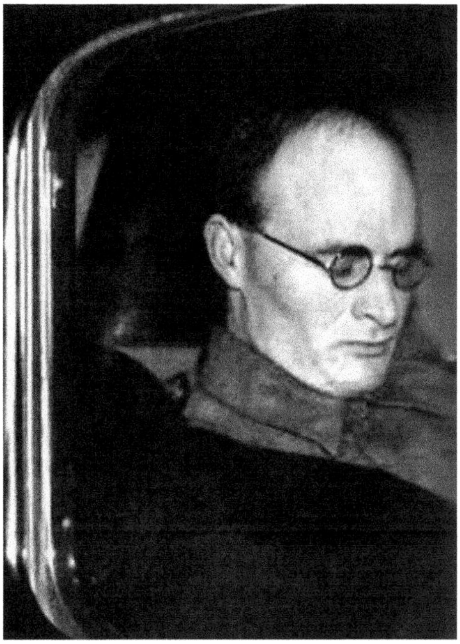

Murderer Harold Hill.

As we have seen, such dreadful and disturbing events can sometimes leave a trace. In 2015, I received a letter from a Mr Tom Reece and his friend Max Hadley. One night after a family party they were travelling home by car from Wycombe. They had decided to go across the county rather than take the main road out of Wycombe. It was past 2.00 a.m. when they were driving along Common Wood Lane towards the village of Penn Street through which their route would take them onto the road to Amersham.

The road was dark and deserted but with occasional mist patches lingering in the hollows and fields. As they rounded a bend in the road the full-beam headlights of the car picked out a strange vision. Standing by the side of the road, on the opposite carriageway, were the unmistakable figures of two children. Mr Reece, who was driving, did not, at first, think it strange. However, as the car neared the children, his friend Mr Hadley sat stiffly up in his seat and exclaimed in an incredulous tone, 'What the hell?' Both men then fixed their eyes on the odd sight as they approached. Mr Reece says they were travelling at about 35–40 mph, and it must have taken about seven seconds for them to first see the kids, register them and then quickly pass. As they did so they saw that the children had their backs to the road and were staring across the field up to a wooded area.

'It all seemed to happen in a flash', Mr Reece reported. 'I was tired and wasn't thinking about anything in particular when I saw the figures. Max sat up and shouted. We both briefly glimpsed at the children as we shot past. They looked completely solid and normal. If it wasn't for the lateness of the hour I wouldn't have thought it odd.'

However, Mr Hadley was of another opinion. When his friend said should we stop and see if they are ok, the reply was a firm 'No. Just drive. Just drive.' Max instinctively knew that what they had seen was not right. He says a cold shiver coursed through him. All he wanted to do was to get the hell out of there. As the car continued on down the lane Mr Reece checked his rear-view mirror, but it was impossible to see anything save the dull red glow from his tail lights.

When they returned home to Amersham both found it hard to sleep. While Max tried to reason the vision from his mind, Mr Reece was of the opinion that they had seen the ghosts of two children.

What is tragic about the murder of two innocent children is that it might never had occurred but for a cruel twist of fate. On the day the girls were abducted they left Tylers Green school at the normal time, 3.45 p.m., and along with other pupils and accompanying parents proceeded homeward. They had got some distance from the school when one of the girls, realising she had forgotten something, asked her friend to return with her to fetch it. Both went back to the classroom, but after twenty minutes of fruitless searching they gave up and once again left the building. By now the other children and parents had dispersed and the two girls walked on alone. When they reached the crossroads at Common Wood Lane they had their fateful meeting with their abductor.

If this dreadful incident was an instance of preordained synchronicity, then it was a cruel, heartless and devastating example. Likewise, what are we to make of three truck crews encountering the same road apparition and then all experiencing engine trouble at the same spot? No doubt all are uncanny incidents. One will bring tears to your eyes; the other will make you scratch your head and search for answers.

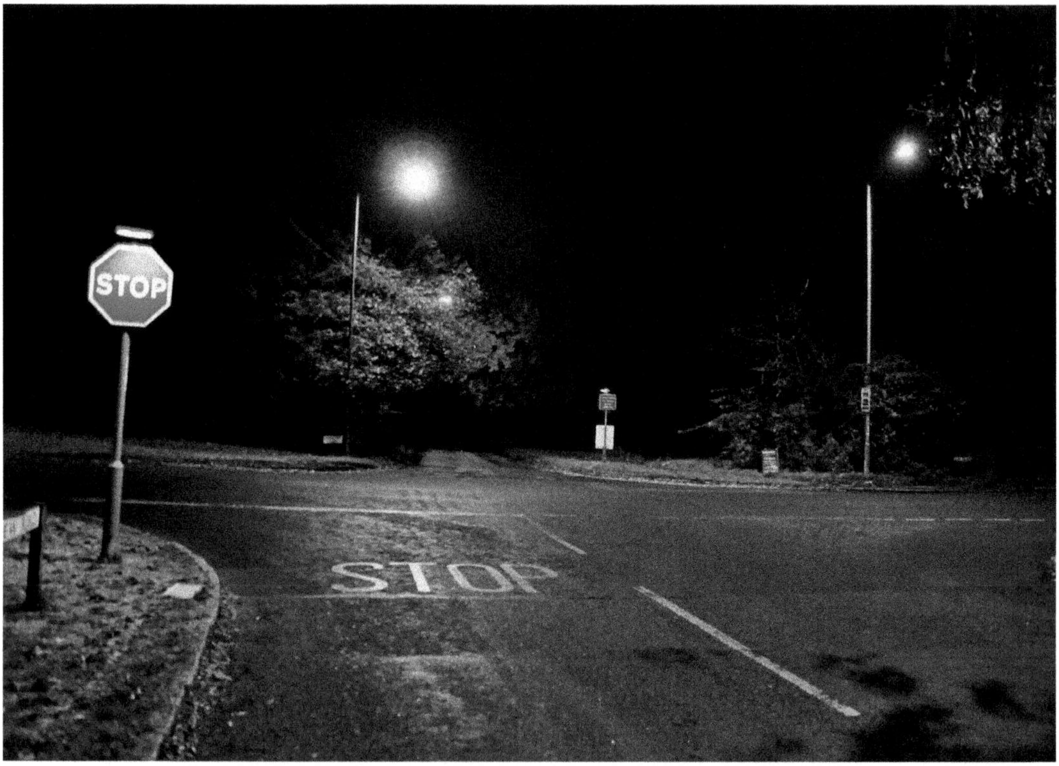

The crossroads where the children were abducted.

The Ghosts of the Prime Ministers' Church

The parish church of St Peter and St Paul, Ellesborough, stands proudly on a steep knoll halfway between the towns of Princes Risborough and Wendover. It was built in the late fourteenth century, but has undergone extensive Victorian restoration. The Hawtry family were once lords of the manor and are laid to rest in the church. They were also the owners of the nearby stately manor house of Chequers. The house was bequeathed by the Hawtrys to the office of British Prime Minister, and is used by the King's first minister as his country residence.

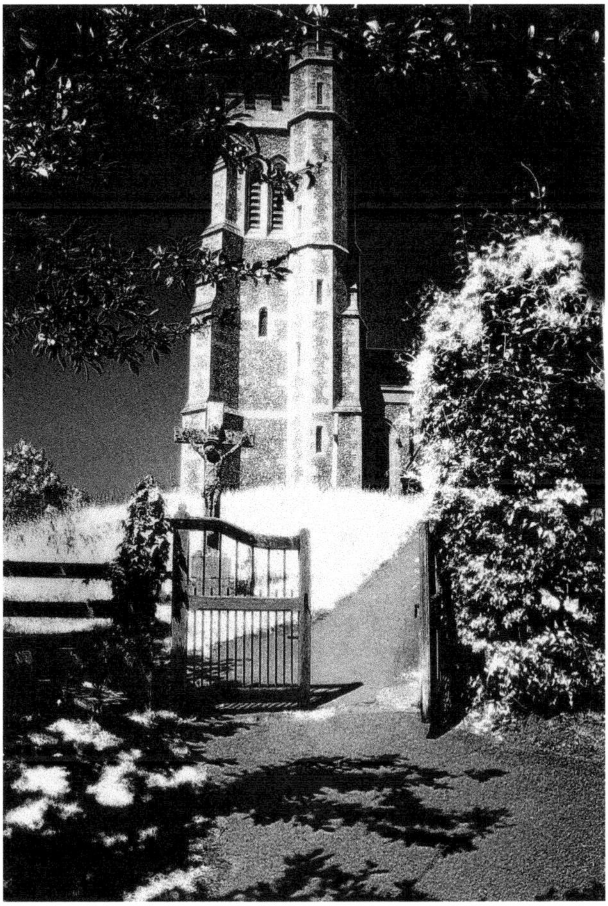

Haunted Ellesborough church.

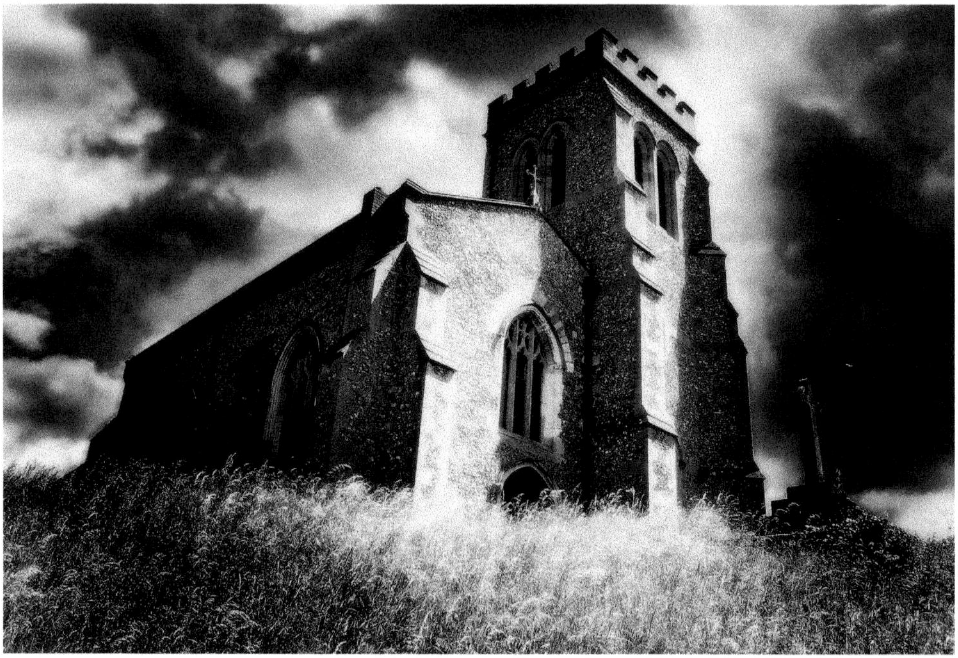

Imposing Ellesborough.

Ellesborough Church is also known as the Prime Ministers' Church, as many Labour or Conservative leaders have attended worship there. Margaret Thatcher prayed at the church during the Falklands conflict.

The church also has its resident ghosts. Over the years the apparition of a tall figure dressed in medieval attire has been seen to glide towards the memorial tablets commemorating the Hawtry family, although it is unclear if it is the ghost of Sir Thomas Hawtry who was lord of the manor in the sixteenth century.

The figures of two women have been seen sitting in the pews nearest the altar, but their identity is unknown. There is also a lady in white. She is said to be the unrequited lover of Revd Robert Wallis, who was rector of the church in the early seventeenth century. The ghost of Wallis himself has been seen on the footpath leading to the south door. One 1980s rector is said to have seen the apparition on several occasions.

The Hughenden Dragon

One of the fascinating aspects of a town's secret history is how time after time myth and partial fact, together with a host of Chinese whispers, are interwoven to become an unsubstantiated belief. A story so preciously traditional it cannot be dismissed or put under the spotlight of logic or rationale. A tale, even though seemingly preposterous, we want to be true. One such story was related to me during the research for this book.

It was whilst I was relaxing with a pint in a local that the barman, knowing of my research in to High Wycombe's secrets, asked if I had ever heard of the 'Hughenden dragon'? No, I had not, but I insisted he related the story. As is the norm in such retelling, the barman could only offer me what scanty details he had heard, and those were probably picked up from someone who himself had been told of the tale from a third party. Nonetheless the story was so intriguing I asked him to tell me all he knew.

Back in the 1920s a mother and her baby were walking in Hughenden Park. The baby was in a pram, and as they neared an ornamental pond or lake a creature rose from the water and tried to attack the mother. She managed to fight it off, yet the thing persisted in its attack and made to lunge at the baby's pram. The barman was not sure what happened next. Either the mother managed to escape or there are some who say the baby was swallowed up by a dragon from the pond.

It is a fantastic tale, and sadly totally preposterous. Such an incident would have had the authorities descend on Hughenden with all manner of weaponry to catch or kill Wycombe's answer to the Loch Ness Monster. However, as is many the case, there might well be a hint of truth in the story. Even the most outlandish folk tale has, at its route, a morsel of fact. For that we must go back to the middle of the eighteenth century.

In October 1758 there appeared in *The Gentleman's Magazine* a letter from an Edgar Bochart relating the story of a water serpent he had come across whilst travelling through Wycombe during the summer. Bochart at first thought the story ridiculous but had sufficient curiosity to seek out a farm where locals informed that the incident was supposed to be depicted on a wall. He went to the farm and on one of its walls found a painting of a dragon-like creature and a pencilled record of its history. The story, which he felt 'in every respect, to be true', is as follows.

A woman of the farm was used to getting water from a nearby pond. In the year 1578, she was troubled by a large water serpent which she frequently saw when she went to get water. The woman was frightened of the creature and told her neighbours about it. A plan was then agreed to do away with the serpent. The woman was to attract the beast by sitting by the pond side, whilst some of her neighbours hid behind the briars that almost surrounded the water, ready to kill the creature. The plan was successful and to mark the event the serpent was stuffed with straw and hung up outside the house.

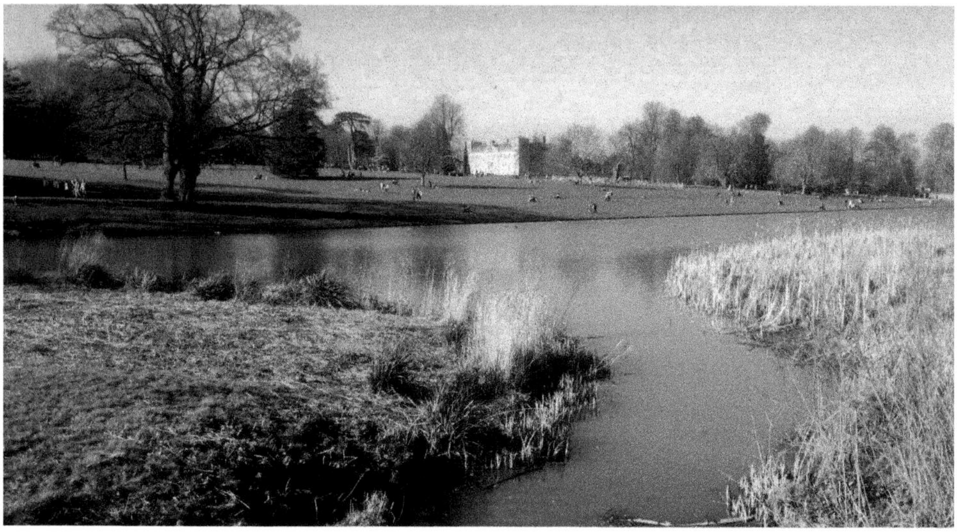

Does a dragon still lurk in Hughenden pond?

Over the years the skin rotted and so a likeness of the creature was painted on a wall of the farm. The painting also gradually deteriorated and so had to be restored from time to time. The likeness Bochart saw showed a creature like a traditional dragon.

The house that contained the dragon painting was described as having 'coats of arms visible in many places' and inferred that it must have been a hospital of the Knights Templar. He also stated that about half a mile in the valley beneath the house was the church of Hitchendon in the county of Bucks, which housed memorials to some of the knights. Hitchendon was the seventeenth- and eighteenth-century name for what is now the parish of Hughenden. What Bochart was referring to was the church of St Michael and All Angels, Hughenden. The dedication is particularly interesting in that St Michael churches are frequently associated with dragon legends.

In the eighteenth century, around half a mile from the church stood the ancient manor house of Rockhalls. In previous centuries this had been the home of the Wellesbourne family who are known to have had a penchant for armorial carvings to such an extant that during the reign of Henry VIII some of the Wellesbournes claimed, without any grounds whatsoever, to be descended from the family of Simon de Montfort, the French nobleman who organised the first English parliament. They even went to the trouble of having fake monuments, supposedly of a De Montfort/Wellesbourne ancestor, made and placed in the chancel aisle at Hughenden church.

Sometime towards the end of the eighteenth century the old Rockhalls was pulled down, but a number of carvings were saved and incorporated in the buildings now known as Rockhalls Farm and Brands Lodge, where they can still be seen today. The armorial carvings identify Rockhalls as the house where Bochart saw the dragon painting. However, it is harder to identify with any certainty the pond in which the dragon was supposed to have lived. One believed site is on the opposite side of the road from Rockhalls Farm, about 100 yards up the road towards Widmer End. However, this pond may only be what remains of the old Rockhalls moat and tends to dry up in the summer. Today it has silted up and is surrounded by bushes and brambles which are very easy to imagine as Bochart's 'briars'.

Now, of course, Rockhalls Farm is situated some way from Hughenden Park, and if the mother, with her baby in the pram, was attacked by a creature in the moat, then it would today be a well-known piece of local folklore. But this seems not to be the case. One nineteenth-century historian referred to the Hughenden dragon as 'one of those absurd stories which have a tendency to retard the human mind in its progress to a rational improvement, and which are therefore to be discountenanced by every friend of historical truth'.

Nonetheless, although the dragon story was dismissed as a fairy tale by many, there are some local people who can recall a particular pond in the vicinity of old Rockhalls which certainly held a fear for anyone passing by it. When the story of the dragon first appeared in a local paper it prompted correspondence from an elderly lady who had heard the tale of the serpent when she was a child. Her father had told her of a woman and baby being swallowed up by a dragon from a pond located somewhere between Terries and Four Ashes. The pond was said to be reached by a footpath off the Kingshill Road, and reputed to have been where Simon de Montfort had his castle. Although there is no evidence pointing to De Montfort's castle, today there is still a small moat and a deep ditch said to date from about the twelfth century – the same date as when Hughenden church was built.

The pond indicated by the lady would appear to have been the same as the one referred to by Bochart. Undoubtedly local tradition, and the gloomy nature of the pond and its overgrown surroundings, had distorted the story into one of a woman and baby being swallowed by the beast. It is a suitably spooky and romantic tale for retelling around the winter fire side, and even the most hardened sceptic would surely want it to be true. However, we may not be referring here to a real dragon or serpent, but more probably a symbolic one.

Over the centuries many religious sites have been used continuously, and what was initially a pagan site would in turn become Christian, and eventually a parish church would be constructed at the location. Connecting these sites were said to be a network of ley lines. These lines across the landscape became associated with the ways of the dead. At certain times of the year strange lights and phantom creatures were seen, and where the paths intersected it was believed that supernatural phenomenon was heightened.

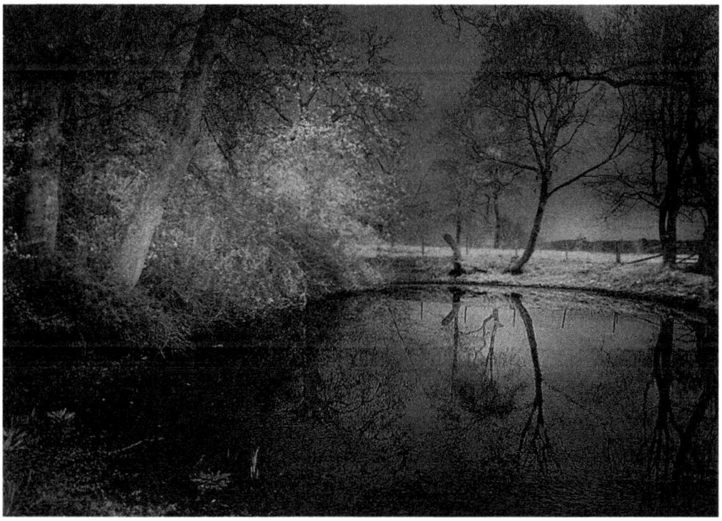

Creepy ponds, the lair of unknown mythical beasts.

Whatever one's views on ley lines are, it has indeed been shown that where they have been mapped an unusually high number of paranormal incidents have been recorded. Moreover, these lines were also known as 'Dragon Paths'. The idea and force of the dragon or serpent was intrinsically connected to the scared and supernatural power of the site. Such an ancient British link would have no doubt lasted down the centuries until the Anglo-Saxons arrived in the country.

The Anglo-Saxons were initially pagans, yet, in the year 597, Pope Gregory sent St Augustine to England to convert the bloodthirsty heathens to Christianity. Included in his remit was to replace those old heretical beliefs with Christian teaching as a sign that the old ways were being superseded by a far more powerful doctrine. The emergence of Christianity also included symbolic subservience and a replacing of pagan icons with Christian ones.

When the first Christian place of worship was established at Hughenden it is possible the builders might well have been aware of the area's heathen past and its dragon path associations. Therefore, what better person to dedicate the building to than the biblical slayer of dragons, St Michael. Such a dedication would have signified that Christianity had triumphed over paganism and the supernatural beliefs of the heathens.

The power of time and the centuries, together with the passing down of folklore, to distort and add to ancient tales is common all over Britain. The account of the Hughenden dragon, and its slaying by the locals, which Edgar Bochart came across 200 years ago, and which dated back even further, may well be the ever-changing narrative of a tradition whose origins are now so remote as to be lost forever.

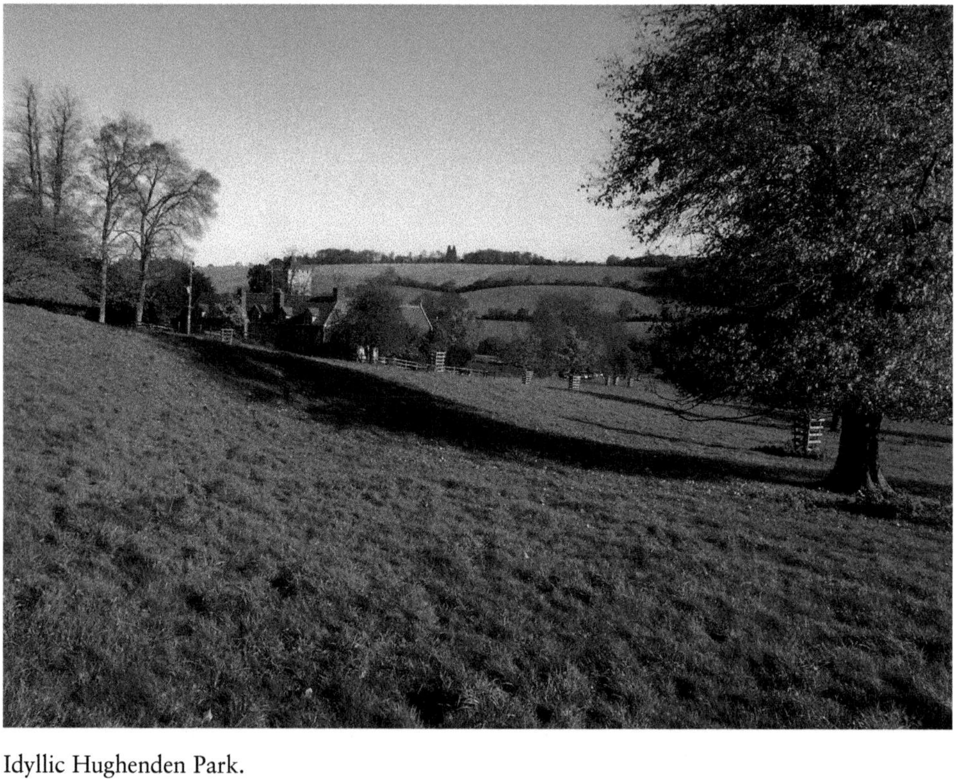

Idyllic Hughenden Park.

The Ghost of Disraeli

Mythical dragons aside, Hughenden is also famous for its political associations. Hughenden Manor stands just outside the centre of High Wycombe, and today is mostly known as the former home of Victorian politician and statesman Benjamin Disraeli, who lived there from 1847 till his death in 1881. The manor of Hughenden is first recorded in 1086, and although not certain, it is possible that a house occupied the site in the fifteenth century. During the sixteenth and seventeenth centuries it was the property of the Dormer family. However, from 1737 it was owned by the Savage family, who began to develop an existing farmhouse in to a modest house of three storeys.

In 1847 the house was purchased by Disraeli, who was a favourite of Queen Victoria. He became Prime Minister in 1868, and again between 1874 and 1880. The statesman remodelled the exterior and interior manor in the Gothic style, although the exterior is in a mock Jacobean brickwork.

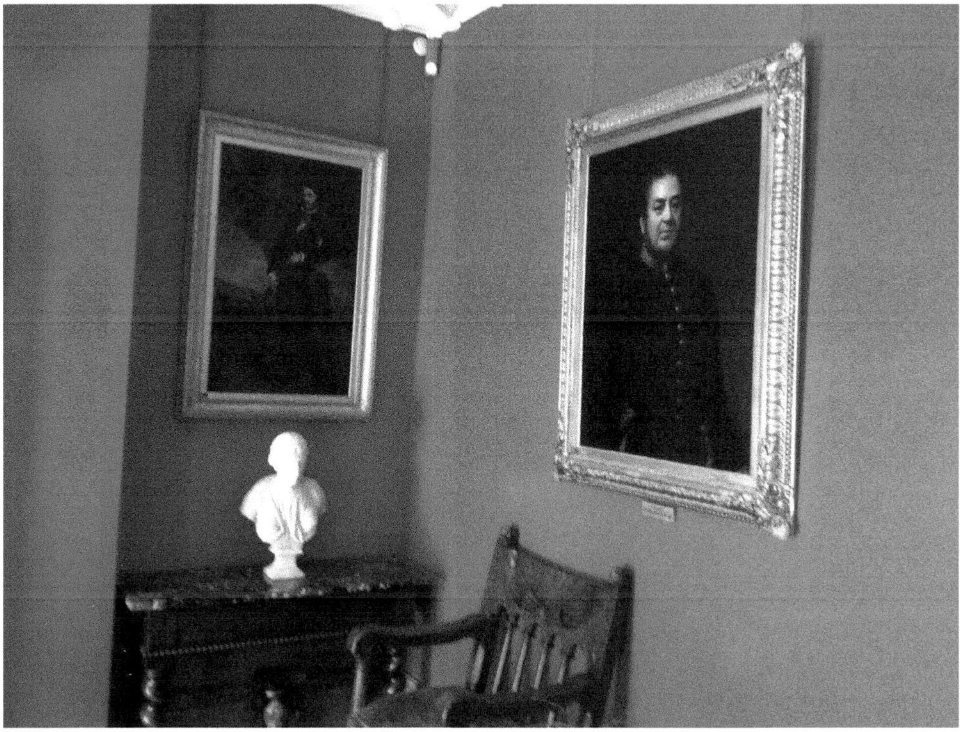

Hughenden interior.

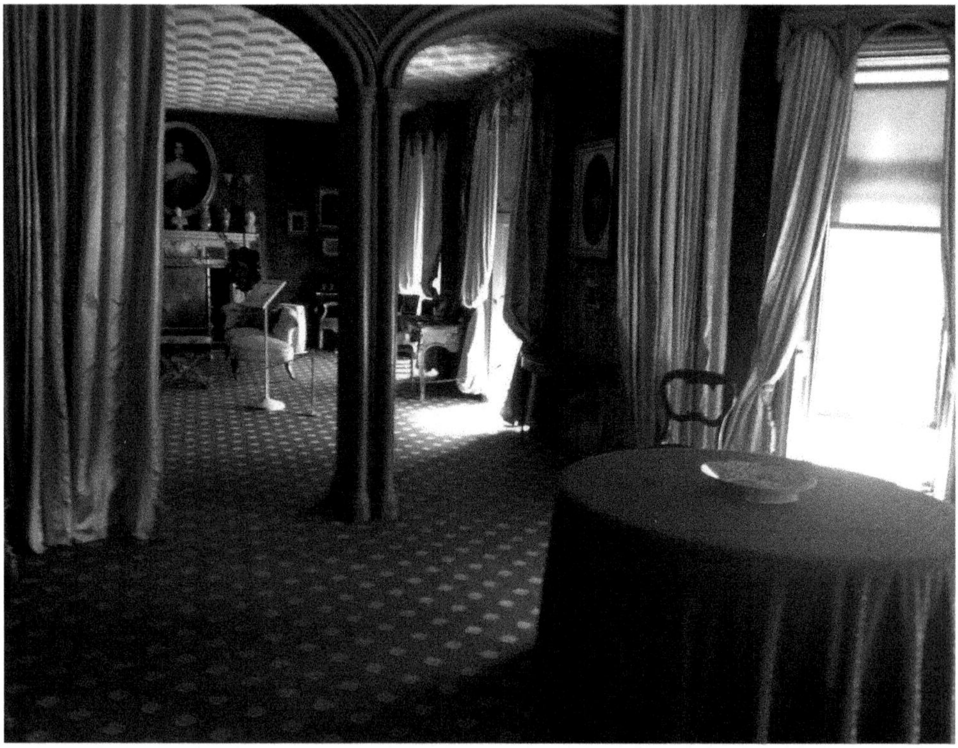

Drawing room, Hughenden Manor.

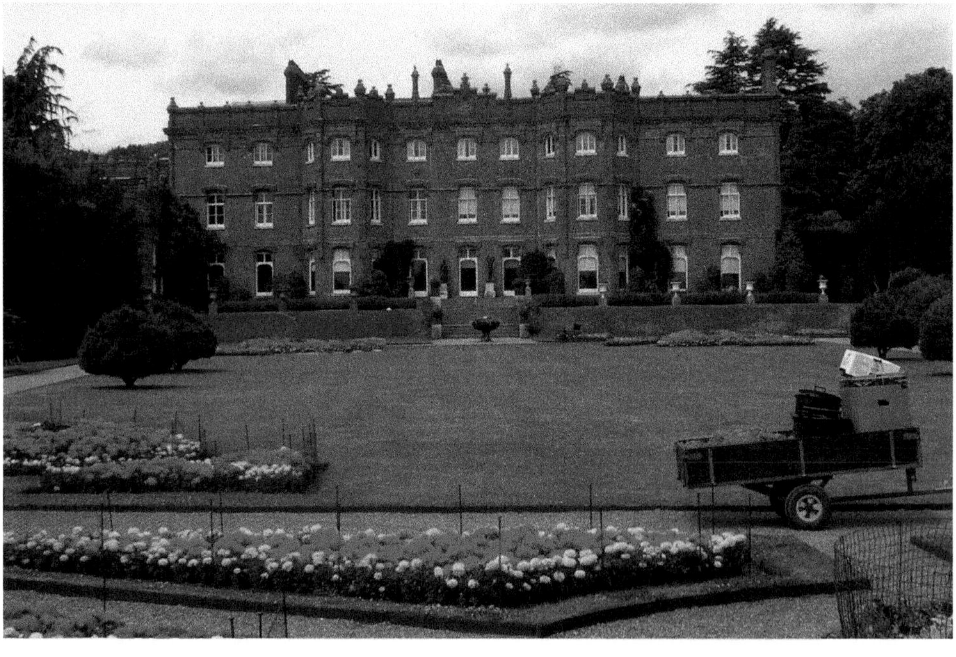

Hughenden Manor.

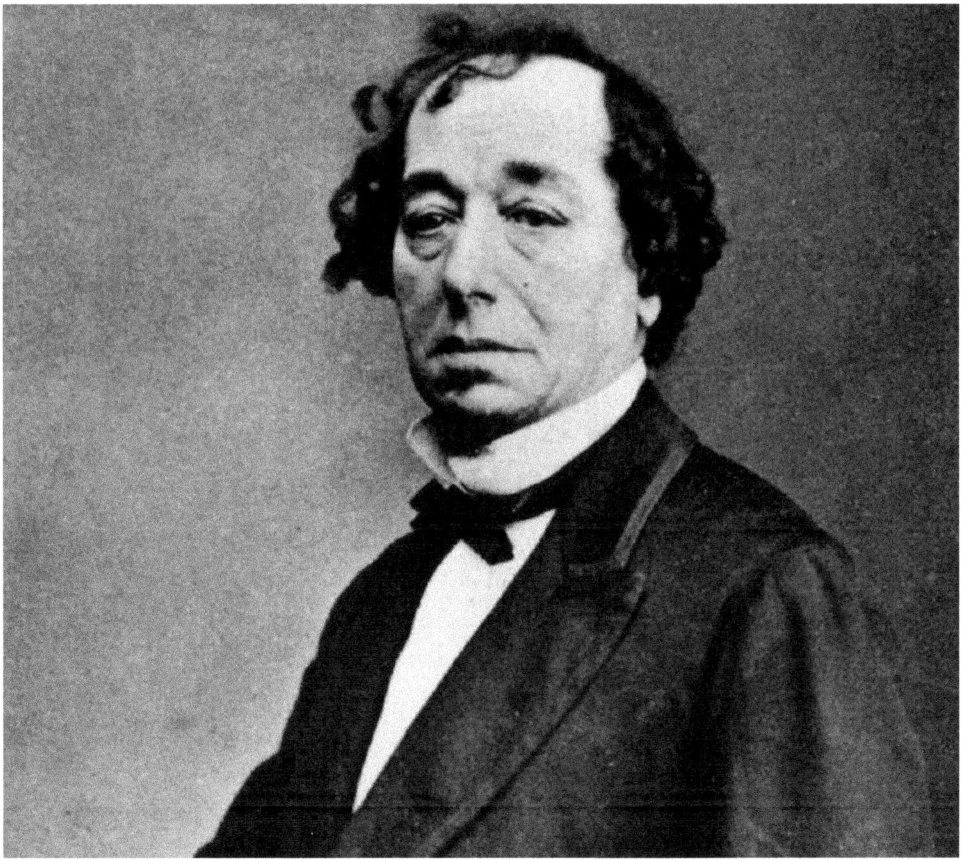

Does the ghost of Disraeli haunt Hughenden?

The house interior underwent many changes after the politician's death, but several rooms have been restored, with many of Disraeli's personal belongings and mementoes displayed as they would have been during his lifetime.

During the Second World War, the house was used as a secret intelligence base code-named 'Hillside', where air ministry staff analysed aerial photography of Germany and created maps for bombing missions, including the famous Dambusters raid in 1943. The house is also said to be haunted by Disraeli's ghost.

It was soon after his death that the apparition of the Victorian politician was seen walking the rooms and staircase of Hughenden Manor. During a visit to the house by the ghost club, one of its members reported that while looking at a painting in a side room, she caught movement out of the corner of her eye. Turning, she saw the ghost of Disraeli staring at her. He stood for a few seconds before dissolving into nothing.

Paranormal aromas have been experienced at the manor. In his time the former politician was looked upon as something of a dandy, and would often wear perfume or cologne. Several staff members have reported that they have entered rooms and smelt an overwhelming fragrance.

Suicide Room

In the summer of 1976, eighteen-year-old Linda Adam was offered a place at the University of Buckingham to study English. At the time there was a shortage of accommodation on the university campus, and the new student was required to take lodgings in a Victorian house which had been converted to flats on the edge of the town.

The bedsit was a small affair with a bedroom, tiny kitchen and bathroom. It was furnished with a single bed, table, chairs and a rather large, gloomy wardrobe which stood in a corner.

Linda soon settled into her new lodgings, and made friends with her fellow students. However, some weeks later, she began to wake in the middle of the night to hear the sound of heavy breathing in the small room. She recalls it was not the sounds of man, but rather the rapid inhaling and exhaling of a young person in great distress. Alarmed, she immediately switched on her bedside lamp. The room was empty, and the sound had ceased.

The sound of heavy breathing occurred only intermittently afterwards. Yet, there was one other strange occurrence which puzzled her. Each morning she awoke to find the door of the bulky wardrobe standing open. No matter how she secured the door, it would always be swung back.

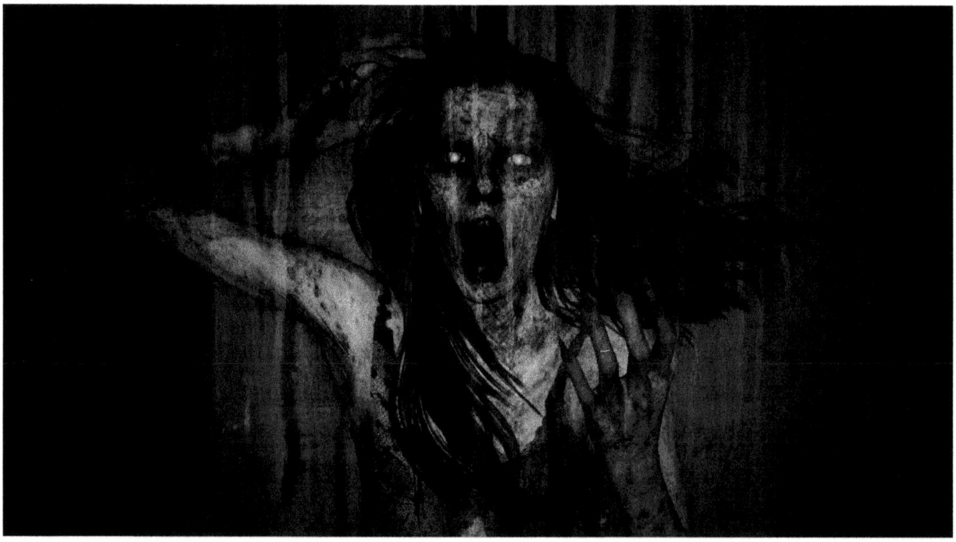

Is this what Linda Adam saw emerge from her wardrobe? (David Saunderson)

Linda began to become more concerned about the wardrobe when she discovered a key to the door and locked it. Yet, in the morning, much to her alarm, she found the door open and the key lying on the linoleum floor.

The student now seriously considered moving out of the bedsit, but she knew that might jeopardize her place at the university. A few nights later that decision was made for her.

She had been out with friends and returned to her bedsit after midnight. She was tired and went straight to bed. She cannot recall the time but she was awoken in the small hours by the same rapid breathing she had heard when she had first moved in.

Leaning over to the bedside table she felt for the light switch, but the light did not come on. Sitting up, she looked over to the wardrobe. The door was open. Much to her terror, Linda could just make out the shape of a figure within. The young student now became almost paralyzed with fear as she saw someone step out of the wardrobe and move towards the bed. It was all too much for the terrified girl, and with one swift movement she leapt from the bed and ran screaming to her fellow students.

Linda, unsurprisingly, moved out of the room. She was later to discover that she wasn't the only student to have experienced the phenomena. It was a sad tale.

Five years earlier a young female student had been allocated the bedsit. Her anxiety about completing her studies and gaining a degree plagued her night and day. She was a chronic asthmatic and suffered crippling depression. One morning she didn't show up for a lecture. Friends became concerned when she had been absent for a week. The university authorities had to force the bedsit door. The poor girl was found in the wardrobe, her wrists cut.

P. S. After the experience of Linda Adam, I believe the wardrobe was removed and burned.

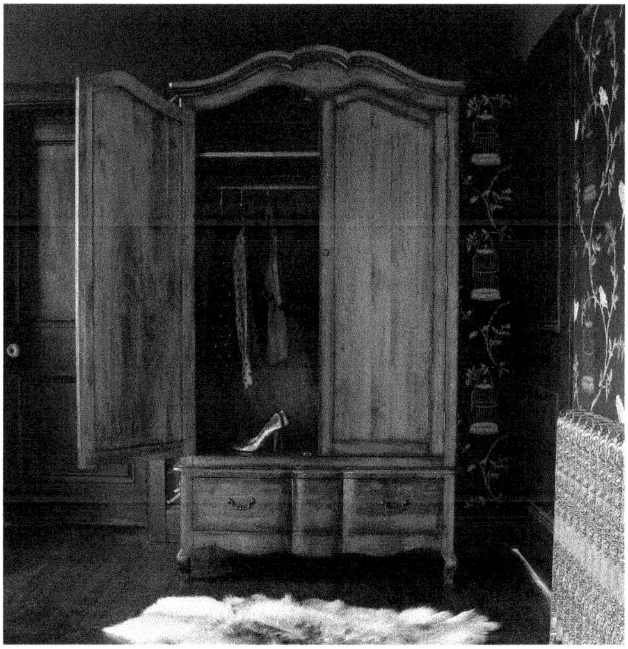

The haunted wardrobe.

The Mystery of Sleepy Cottage

The next time you watch an episode of *The Vicar of Dibley*, staring Dawn French, consider this curious incident which occurred in 'Sleepy Cottage' in the quiet Chiltern village of Turville in the late nineteenth century.

Despite its peace and tranquillity, Turville was the site of a curious and baffling nineteenth-century mystery. In 1871, eleven-year-old Ellen Sadler purportedly fell asleep and did not wake for nine years. The case attracted widespread attention and for a time the village and Ellen became a tourist attraction. She was admitted to hospital, but after four months her condition was declared incurable, and she was sent home.

Ellen's celebrity grew and her family made considerable money from visitors' donations. As the years progressed with no sign of Ellen's waking, speculation grew

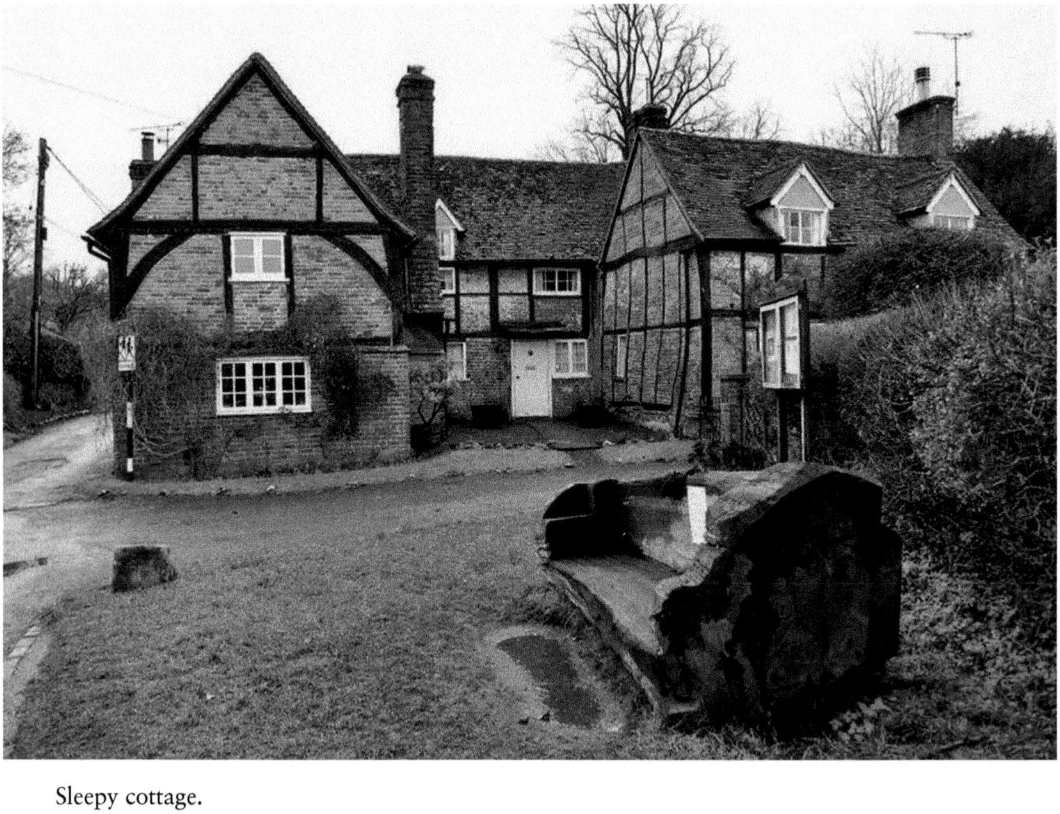

Sleepy cottage.

that her illness was either a hoax or caused by her mother. Others claimed it was the actions of a local witch who had enchanted the poor girl.

By March 1873, Ellen was believed to be suffering from starvation. At first, she had largely subsisted on port, tea and milk. After about fifteen months, while her mother was attempting to administer arrowroot, Ellen's jaw locked closed forcing her parents to sustain her with 'wine and gruel using the spout of a toy teapot inserted between two broken teeth'.

Soon scepticism of Ellen's illness began to grow, for it was said that villagers sometimes saw her sitting, smiling by her window at night. Nevertheless, every effort was made to discover the deception, if any – but without success.

Ellen's mother, Anne, died in May 1880. Five months later, in November, Ellen awoke and had fully recovered. She was twenty-one and claimed to remember nothing of the previous nine years. In 1886 she married and went on to have six children.

The case of Ellen Sadler has remained part of Turville folklore, spawning tales of witchcraft and spirit possession.

The Mad Vicar of Water Stratford

The village of Water Stratford, 2 miles west of Buckingham, would seem to be the last place one would think of escaping to in the advent of a prophetic, fiery Armageddon. Yet, this sleepy Bucks backwater was, in 1690, besieged by a deluge of fanatical disciples convinced that it was the only place on Earth which would be spared the ending of the world.

In 1674 John Mason became parish priest of St Giles at Water Stratford. He was a puritan and was much admired by his fellow clergy. He was a man of gentle disposition and moderate views, but he turned to Calvinism. One of its beliefs was that salvation is preordained and that God has chosen from eternity those who are to be saved regardless of how devout and spotless a life one leads on Earth.

In 1690 the good priest was hit by three successive personal blows. A scripture chronology he had worked on for years was rejected by the church authorities and he grieved over his wasted time. Secondly, his closest friend died, and this blow was devastatingly followed by the death of his beloved wife.

Overnight, John Mason became a changed man. He began to experience strange dreams, nightmares and delusions which haunted his waking hours. His preaching began to take on an alarming dimension. On Sunday mornings he would thunder forth from his pulpit that he was the prophet and miracle worker Elijah, and that he could summon up the dead and bring down fire from Heaven.

Unsurprisingly, Mason's superiors in the church began to get a little concerned. Not so his parishioners. Hundreds of people from the surrounding area descended on the Buckinghamshire village eager to hear the word of the new messiah. So great was the impassioned multitude that there became no room in the church and the crowds packed into the churchyard to listen to Mason as he addressed the throng from one of the church windows.

Eventually the church authorities sent the Revd Maurice, Rector of Tyringham, a close friend of Revd Mason, to Water Stratford to report on what was happening. On his arrival he found the village in pandemonium. Throughout the rectory, men, woman and children were running up and down the stairs bellowing, laughing and clapping as if the day of judgment was just around the corner.

Whilst Mason's followers danced themselves into euphoria, he lay in a garret at the top of the house dying. He died a month later prophesying that he would be resurrected in three days. It was thought that his passing would put an end to the madness. However, it was not to be, as three days after the revd had been laid to rest the multitude still remained in the village, and the din of singing and chanting continued as they waited for Mason to rise from his coffin.

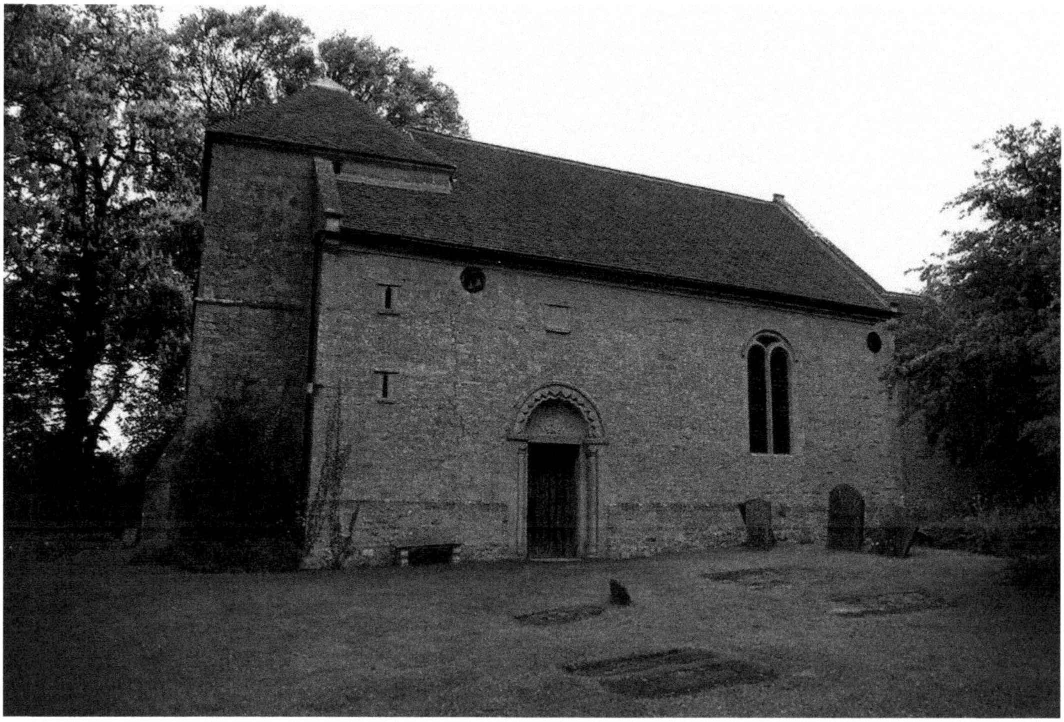

Water Stratford church.

In desperation Mason's successor, the Revd Rushworth, opened up the rector's grave and displayed the corpse to show one and all that their leader was indeed stone dead. Incredibly there were some who still believed that Revd Mason would put in an appearance and they hung around the churchyard for up to sixteen years. Eventually they were dispersed by the army.

There is a curious and uncanny coda to this strange story. Revd Mason prophesised that he would be resurrected from his grave three days after his burial. Perhaps he got the timing wrong. In the summer of 2016 two tourists, who were returning from visiting the magnificent gardens at Stow House just 3 miles away, passed through Water Stratford and decided to take a look at the church. It was a beautiful summer's afternoon. They knew nothing of the church's history or the shenanigans of Revd Mason. They were about to enter the building when both heard shouting coming from inside. They hesitated in opening the south door thinking that there was some kind of altercation occurring. The ranting seemed to last some thirty seconds, at times loud, and then fading to a mumble, as if a person was reading the Bible through a faulty loud hailer. Eventually it ceased and all was silent.

The two ladies decided to gingerly open the door and peep inside. The building was as quiet as could be. They made their way into the church, but it was totally deserted. Had Revd Mason put in his prophesised appearance? If it was not the good reverend, then perhaps his followers still frequent the churchyard waiting for him to rise up from his grave. Some weeks after the two ladies' experience a young couple were driving through Water Stratford late at night when they heard what they assumed to be a rave or pop concert happening nearby. Both heard the unmistakable sound of hordes of people singing and chanting. There was the banging of drums and the screams of what they thought to be appreciative fans.

Yet there were no festival lights illuminating the area or glowing in the distance. The couple thought nothing more of it and drove on. But some days later a chance remark to a villager regarding the pop concert was met with blankness. There was no event, and there never has been in Water Stratford. It would have been surely noticed.

It is unclear whether or not the four people who had heard the sounds later became aware of the history of Revd John Mason and his devout followers. If so, they would have no doubt put it down to being the ghosts of the reverend and his phantom disciples. But from the nature of the phenomena, it would seem that Mason had not risen from the dead, but rather his mad church ranting and the racket of his flock were the result of the phenomena we call the stone tape – playable only to those who are fortunate to be in the right place at the right time. No doubt back in 1690 the reverend and his followers made enough din for the sounds to be heard 300 years later, and who knows, still be audible in 2390.

The Haunting of West Wycombe

The village of West Wycombe lies about 2 miles from the centre of High Wycombe. It is a pleasing location containing many fine half-timbered buildings dating from the fifteenth to eighteenth centuries, and even though today it is somewhat marred by the traffic which thunders along its high street, the alleys, lanes and courtyards off the main thoroughfare still retain an air of quiet calm. Yet, it is here, in this rural charm, that ghosts, murder, pagan worship and the debauchery of eighteenth-century titled gentry are all inextricably linked with this seemingly, peaceful English village.

West Wycombe could well be described as a place perfect for ghosts and the mysteries of Britain's pagan past. The hilltop parish church, dedicated to St Lawrence, the patron saint of prostitutes, stands within the ramparts of an Iron Age hill fort. The site has been continuously occupied for thousands of years. A Bronze Age settlement is widely believed to have first existed on the hill, and research has shown that a pagan temple was constructed in a similar style to Stonehenge. The Romans also built their own settlement and religious temple here. The hill retained its religious importance and the first Christian church was erected in AD 635.

With such an ancient and dark past it seems appropriate that the one man who would become Lord of the Manor at West Wycombe took eagerly to the pleasures, rituals and rakish delights of eighteenth-century decadence.

In 1724, Sir Francis Dashwood (1708–81), 2nd Baronet, and later 15th Baron le Despencer, succeeded to the estate and set about remodelling the house of West Wycombe Park. Like many titled gentlemen of his day, he embarked on the 'Grand Tour' of Europe and returned to England with his own grandiose plans for West Wycombe.

In 1751 the fourteenth-century church of St Lawrence disappeared within Dashwood's rebuilding of the interior copied on the third-century temple of the sun at Palmyra near Damascus. Only the medieval tower was retained, which itself was considerably heightened and topped by a great golden ball fitted with benches, and large enough to contain six people. It was in the golden ball that Dashwood and his cronies drank the night away as they played cards and related bawdy stories.

Yet, of all Sir Francis grand schemes for West Wycombe perhaps the most ambitious was undertaken between 1748 and 1752 with the extension of a series of ancient chalk tunnels under West Wycombe hill into an elaborate labyrinth of caves and chambers.

The caves' design were much inspired by Dashwood's travels in the Mediterranean. The descent through the passageways and underground chambers concluded by crossing a subterranean river named the Styx and entering into the inner temple which is said to lie directly 300 feet below the church of St Lawrence. According to Greek mythology, the River Styx separated the mortal world from the immortal world, and

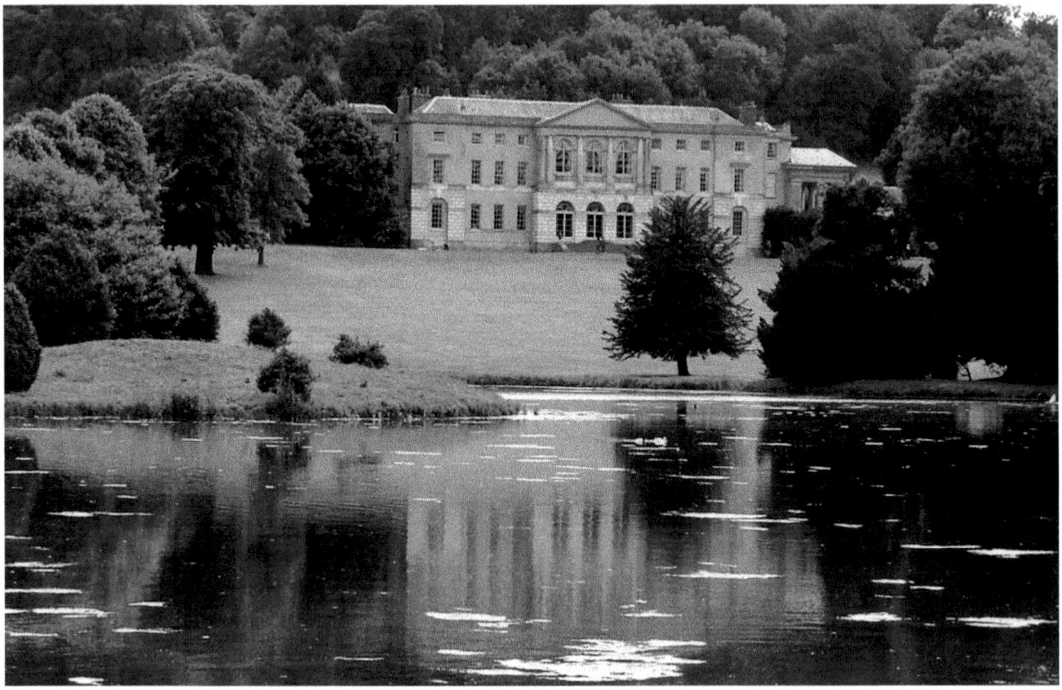

West Wycombe Park.

the subterranean position of the Inner Temple directly beneath St Lawrence's Church was supposed to signify Heaven and Hell.

Between 1750 and 1766 what would become known as the Hellfire Club held its nefarious meetings in the caves below the hill. Here members called themselves the Brothers of St Francis, and their numbers included artist William Hogarth, political activist John Wilkes, John Montague, 4th Earl of Sandwich, poet Paul Whitehead and possibly, at times, American Benjamin Franklin. They greeted each other as 'Brother' and dressed as monks, while their accompanying ladies were attired as virginal nuns. They are said to have conducted satanic or pagan rituals and indulged in drinking, gambling and whoring.

The Hellfire Club disbanded in recrimination in 1766 following a practical jape played on the Earl of Sandwich during one of their drunken ceremonies, and his subsequent ridicule for believing that the materialisation of a monkey, jokingly released from a box by a fellow member, was the manifestation of the Devil.

Following Dashwood's death in 1781, the caves fell out of use and became derelict. It was in the early nineteenth century that the subterranean passageways and West Wycombe hill became the site of reported ghostly phenomena. The spirit Paul Whitehead, a steward and secretary of the Hellfire Club and close friend of Sir Francis Dashwood, is believed to haunt the caves.

The apparition of a man in eighteenth-century clothing has been reported roaming the caves and also ramparts of the Iron Age hill fort which surrounds the Dashwood Mausoleum. A young girl visiting the caves became separated from her friends and found herself alone in a deep part of the labyrinth. Not seeing or hearing any other person, she began to feel lost and frightened. The atmosphere within was changing, becoming cold and dim.

Feeling that she must find her way to the exit, she quickly returned along a passageway which seemed to ascend towards the entrance. She had only gone a short distance when she became aware that someone was following her. Turning, she saw the figure of a man in eighteenth-century clothing standing some distance away staring at her. As they faced each other, the young woman said she felt in no way threatened by the man, and assumed he was one of the cave's living history guides. Yet, as she looked the figure gradually faded away.

Perhaps the most well-known and frequently sighted ghost to walk the caves, and the George and Dragon pub in the village, is that of Suki, an attractive sixteen-year-old barmaid employed at the pub during the late eighteenth century. It was said that she fell for the charms of a gentleman who was passing through the village, much to the annoyance of three local lads who also had their eye on the pretty serving girl.

A message, purporting to be from the handsome gentleman was sent to Suki at the tavern instructing her to meet him in the caves at night. Dressed in her finest white dress, she entered the caves only to find that the message had been a hoax planned by the three jealous boys. In anger, she threw rocks at the laughing lads. When the boys responded by throwing back, Suki was knocked unconscious. She was secretly brought back to her room at the inn but the next morning was found dead. Her ghost is said to walk the corridors of the George and has also been reported to glide across the garden.

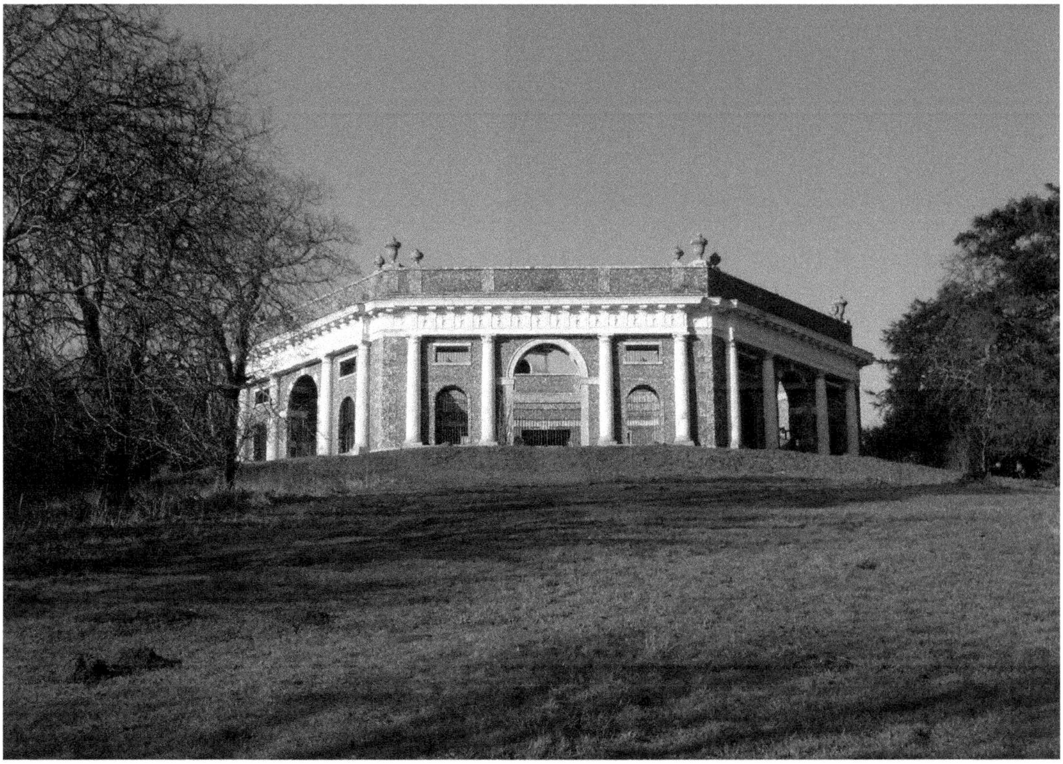

Dashwood mausoleum.

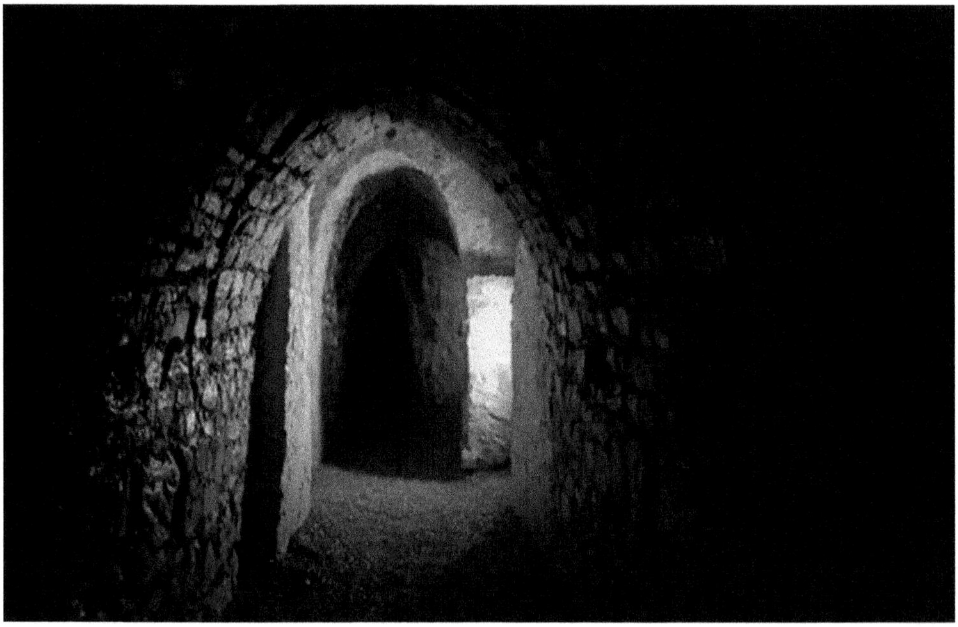

West Wycombe caves.

In 1967 an American tourist staying at the George was intrigued by the story of the ghostly barmaid and wanted to sleep in the haunted room. Partway through the night he awoke with a start as icy hands were placed on his forehead. When he turned on the lamp the feeling went away and the room was empty. Then he noticed a pinpoint of light near the door. As he watched it grew in length and width.

It had a strange, opaque, pearly quality and would vanish when he switched the light on, only to reappear when he turned it off. Plucking up courage, he went over to the light, but as soon as he reached it he felt the most intense cold; he couldn't breathe and his limbs felt heavy. Suddenly the illuminated form moved towards him and he leapt back in terror onto the bed, turning on the light as he did so. At once the strange shape vanished. So much was the tourist's fear at what he had experienced he slept no more that night and left early the next morning vowing never to spend another second at the George.

The spectre of Suki has also been seen looking from the windows of the inn waiting and pining for her lost love. In the early 1990s, the landlady of the George entered one of the rooms and saw the apparition of a young woman with a sad, lost expression sitting by the fire. After a few moments, the ghost turned to look at the landlady and then slowly faded away.

The phantom barmaid is not the only ghost said to walk the rooms and corridors at the pub. Disembodied footsteps, which have been heard descending the main staircase, are believed to be the spirit of a visitor to the inn who was robbed and murdered in his room during the eighteenth century.

The paranormal activity at West Wycombe is not only confined to the George and Dragon pub. In 1995 five teenage girls were camping near woodland on West Wycombe hill. At about 1.00 a.m. they were awoken by the sound of what they described as howling, which seemed to surround the tent. The girls listened, terrified, as the strange guttural cry continued for several minutes before suddenly stopping. Yet, their frightening ordeal had not ceased, as following the sound of howling the tent was lit up by flashing lights which shone from outside.

Although extremely alarmed at what was happening, two of the teenagers plucked up enough courage to pull back the flaps to peer outside. At once the flashing lights were extinguished and the hill was in darkness. All the girls now frantically exited the tent to see what was going on, yet, as they did so, the terrifying howling once again started up, but there was nothing to account for the noise.

The strange sounds continued for a few seconds and again abruptly ceased. As the trembling teenagers clung to each other for comfort, their ordeal was to climax in a terrifying vision. At once all heard the approaching heavy thud of a horse in full gallop.

To the young women's astonishment and terror from nowhere appeared the apparition of a headless man riding a white horse, which sped across the field close to where they stood.

The girls watched open-mouthed as the horse and rider continued up the hill.

Even though they could hear the sounds of hooves on earth, the white horse seemed to be galloping a metre above the ground. Just as quickly as the speeding horse had appeared it vanished into the darkness, and the sound of the hooves faded away. The experience was too much for the five teenagers and they speedily broke down their tent and fled.

There is a tradition at West Wycombe that on moonlit nights the ghost of Sir Francis Dashwood rides up the hill on a brilliant white charger. Unlike the rider experienced by the five teenagers, Sir Francis is not without his head as he gallops towards the church of St Lawrence.

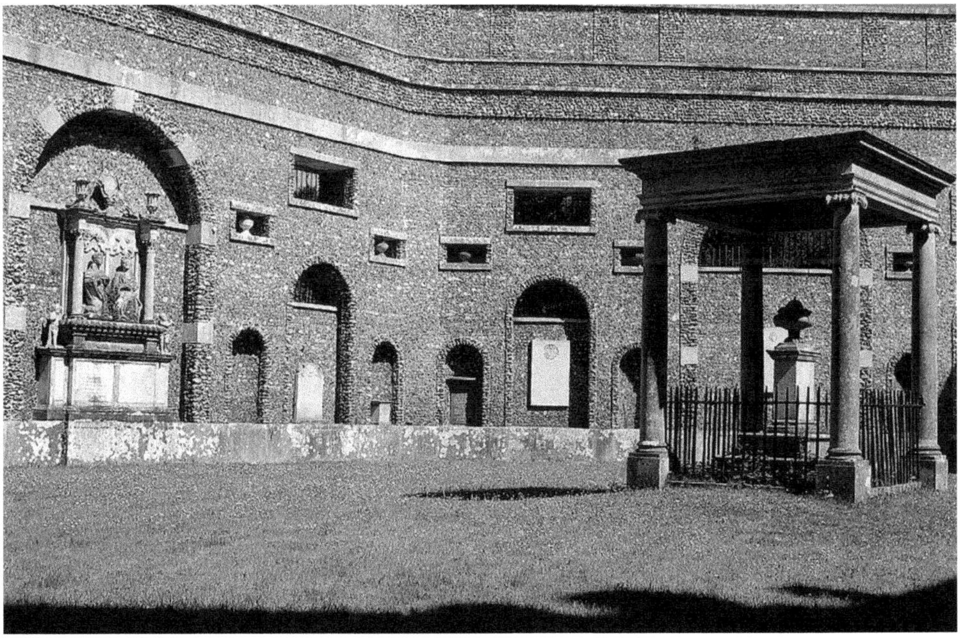

Mausoleum at West Wycombe.

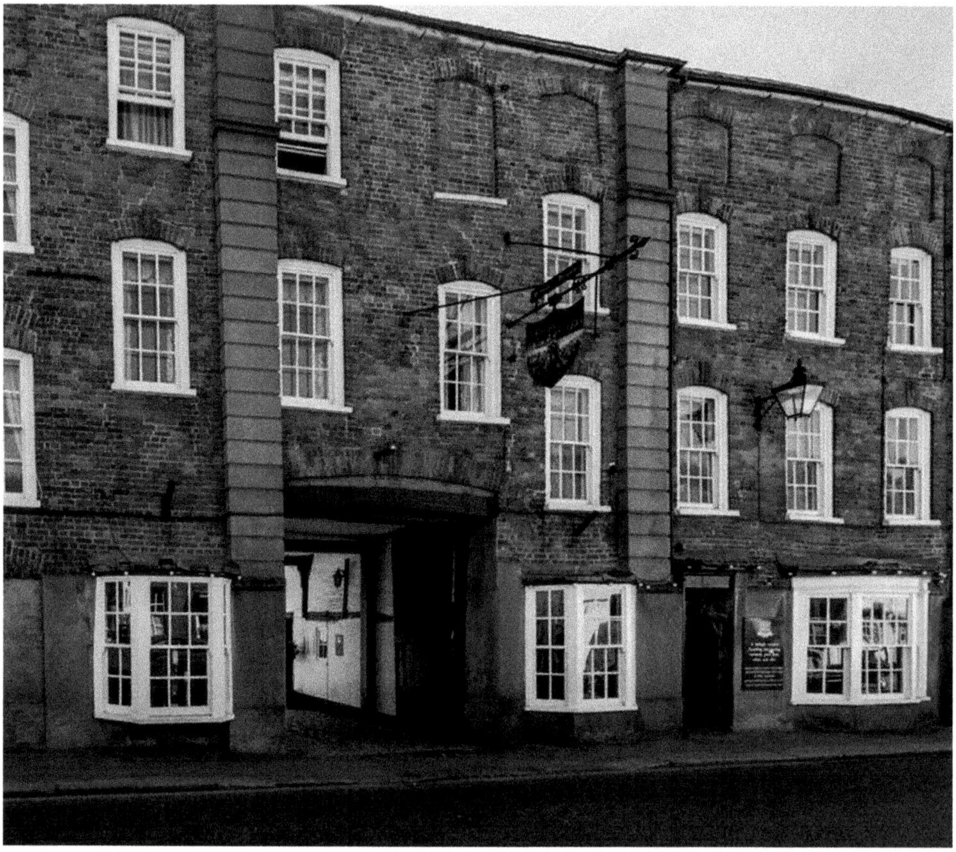

The haunted George Inn in West Wycombe High Street.

Another phantom which has been reported wandering West Wycombe hill and the ramparts of the ancient Iron Age fort is believed to be that of Paul Whitehead. It is said that his ghost haunts the woods surrounding West Wycombe Park. The spectre has been seen waving and beckoning from the trees, and has also been observed outside the house. When Sir Francis Dashwood died in December 1781, the ghost of Whitehead was no longer seen.

West Wycombe House is also not without its ghosts. The music room is said to be haunted by a lady in white who is thought be the grandmother of Sir Francis Dashwood. The ghost of a phantom monk has also been seen in the room.

When celebrated playwright and songwriter Noel Coward was staying at the house he gave a recital in the music room. As he played the piano he saw the figure of a smiling monk watching him. With typical nonchalance and the least hint of alarm, Coward continued his song to the end, where after the smiling, and no doubt appreciative, brother disappeared.

Smiling monks, headless horsemen, ladies in white and phantom barmaids ... West Wycombe would seem to have them all.

Where Frankenstein Was Born

Besides Bram Stoker's blood sucking creation Count Dracula, perhaps the other most well-known fictional monster in literature is Frankenstein, created by Mary Wollstonecraft Shelley in the early nineteenth century. In 1816, Shelly, together with her husband, the poet Percy Bysshe Shelley, and their friend John Polidori were holidaying on the shores of Lake Geneva at the rambling villa Diodati in Switzerland. During their stay the weather was particularly foul with weeks of incessant downpours. Confined to the gloomy, rain-lashed villa, the companions were inspired to compose gruesome blood-curdling tales. It was Mary's composition, inspired by a nightmare, which proved to be the most disquieting, and has since become a classic of Gothic horror. Shelley's tale of the mad Victor Frankenstein and his monstrous creation would ultimately be the inspiration for numerous plays, books and almost a thousand feature films. Two hundred years after its publication it still has the power to frighten and shock. Yet, even though the genesis of Frankenstein was conceived on the romantic shores of a Swiss lake, it was completed in the rather more mundane location of West Street, Marlow.

When the Shelleys returned to England in 1816 they were encouraged to settle in Marlow by the writer Thomas Love Peacock, who would later write his Gothic novel

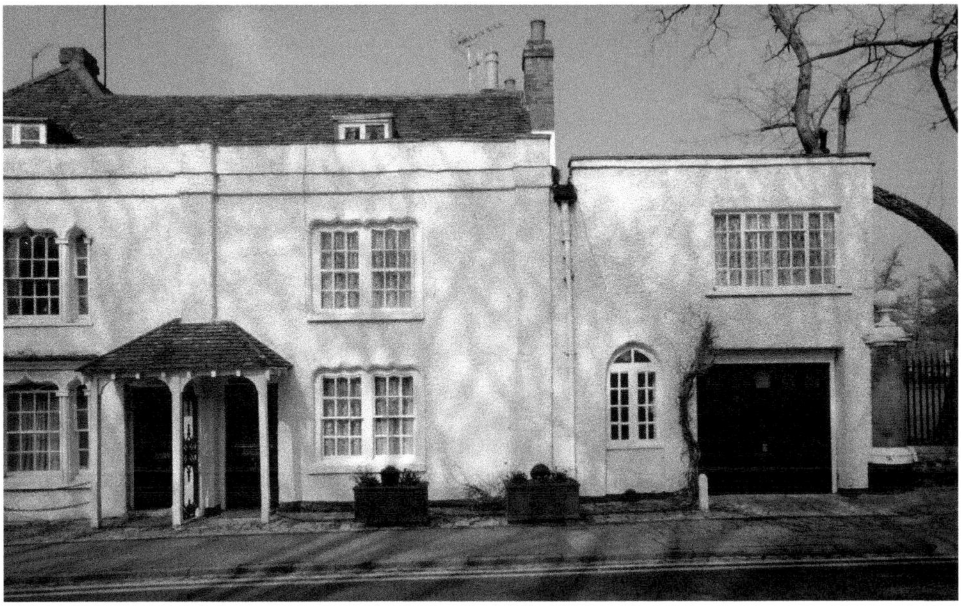

The house in West Street in Marlow where Mary Shelley completed her novel *Frankenstein.*

Nightmare Abbey in a nearby house. Marlow would appear to be a most appropriate location for the completion of Shelley's tale of an insane doctor's desire to create life. In 1758 until his death in 1776, William Battie, an eminent physician specialising in mental illness, lived in Court Garden House. The expression 'batty' is believed to have originated from his work with the mentally ill.

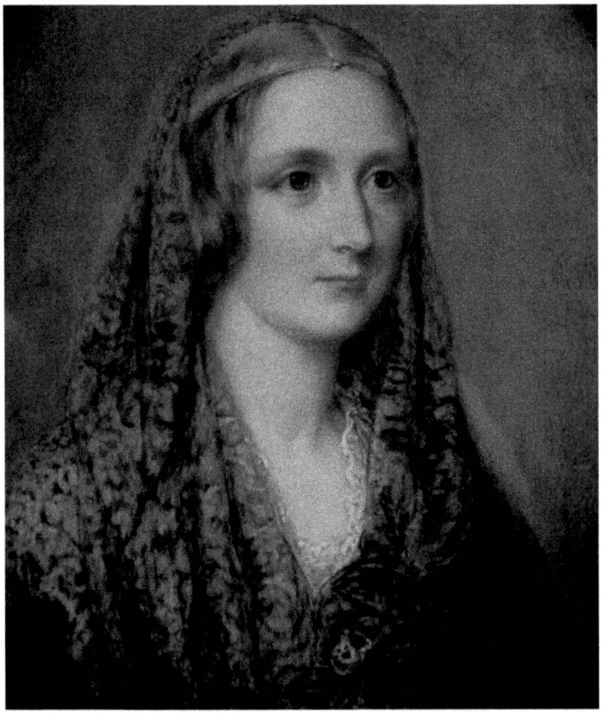

Left: Mary Shelley.

Below: Mary Shelley's creation, Frankenstein's monster. (David Saunderson)

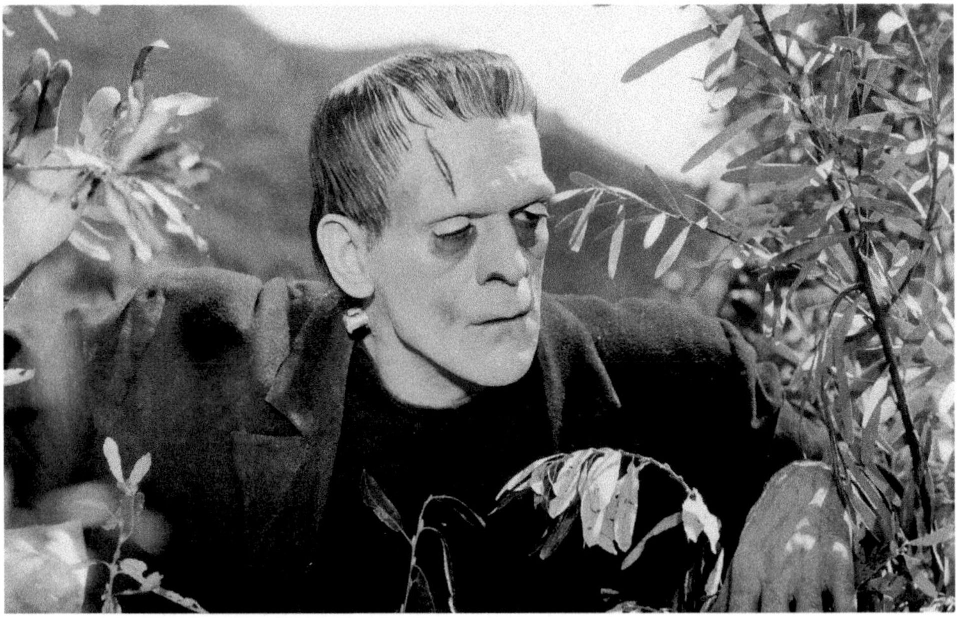

Why Isn't a Hill above Amersham Haunted?

Those who believe in ghosts believe that those places which have seen traumatic and violent death are the locations where a paranormal experience is more likely, the idea being that the agony of the deceased's dreadful end can be, by someone at the right place at the right time, witnessed: the so-called stone tape. Yet a hilltop above the town of Amersham seems to be free of paranormal activity. One wonders why.

It is common knowledge that those found guilty of witchcraft in sixteenth- and seventeenth-century England suffered death by being burned at the stake. However, many witches, mostly women, who were accused of being in league with the horned one were either hanged, drowned, strangled or had their tongues pulled out; between 1440 and 1650 only three women convicted of witchcraft were burnt, and they were first strangled before being set ablaze.

Ironically, in England, those who went to the stake were not disciples of Satan, but in fact devout followers of Christ. And they were set alight by other equally staunch Christians. It was all over the trifling matter of who could own and read the Bible.

The Protestant reformation had caused a religious schism throughout a mainly Catholic Europe. What had started as a protest against the corruption of the Catholic Church soon began to take tackle wider issues, one of which was the translation of the Bible into English. This was strongly rejected by the established Church of the day, as it was feared the word of God could be understood by the ordinary man in the street, and scripture might be interpreted differently from the views of the Church authorities and those who were seen as the traditional intermediaries between man and God – namely priests, bishops and cardinals.

In the early sixteenth century, Amersham, in the south of Bucks, was a hotbed of Lollardism. The name Lollard was a contemptuous term for a follower of John Wycliffe, a fourteenth-century theologian, reformer, translator of the Bible into English and a vigorous attacker of the abuses of the Church of Rome. Wycliffe had many opinions on the way the Church should be run but his main objection was that it was forbidden to read or possess the Bible in an English translation. When Henry IV usurped the throne in 1399 he passed a statute which gave authority to the bishops to punish those who were dissenters. If people were found guilty of heresy, which included owning and reading a Bible in English, they would be condemned to be burned at the stake. Amersham saw a dozen or more people connected with the Lollard movement executed between 1414 and 1532. In 1414 four men from Amersham and one from Great Missenden were executed for adhering to Wycliffe's heretical views. Curiously, Wycliffe himself died peacefully in 1384, but his followers were to be subject to much persecution which would eventually result in the Reformation of the Church.

The Lollards referred to themselves as the Justfast Men' or 'Known Men', because of their steadfast allegiance to God. However, following the executions of the Amersham men, things became quiet, and many of Wycliffe's supporters were forced into hiding.

Around 1500 there was a Lollard revival in the Chilterns, and while most sympathisers recanted their beliefs, others refused and went to the stake. Among those charged and found guilty was William Tylsworth of Amersham. He refused to recant, and in 1506 was sentenced to be burned to death. The savagery of the time, and the hatred felt towards dissenters, is reflected in the fact that Tylsworth's daughter, Joan, was made to light the fire herself.

Other Amersham Lollards who suffered martyrdom for their beliefs were Robert Cosin, burned at Buckingham in 1506; Thomas Chase, strangled and beaten to death in a wood near Wooburn in 1514; and Thomas Mann, burned at the stake in London in 1518.

In 1521 John Longland was appointed Bishop of Lincoln and Confessor to King Henry VIII. To gain favour with his new royal master, a fresh round of heresy trials was embarked upon. In that same year six men and one woman from Amersham were put on trial in St Mary's Church. None recanted their belief that they had the right to read and interpret the holy scripture and to worship God according to their conscience. They were found guilty and taken from the church to a hill high above the town where

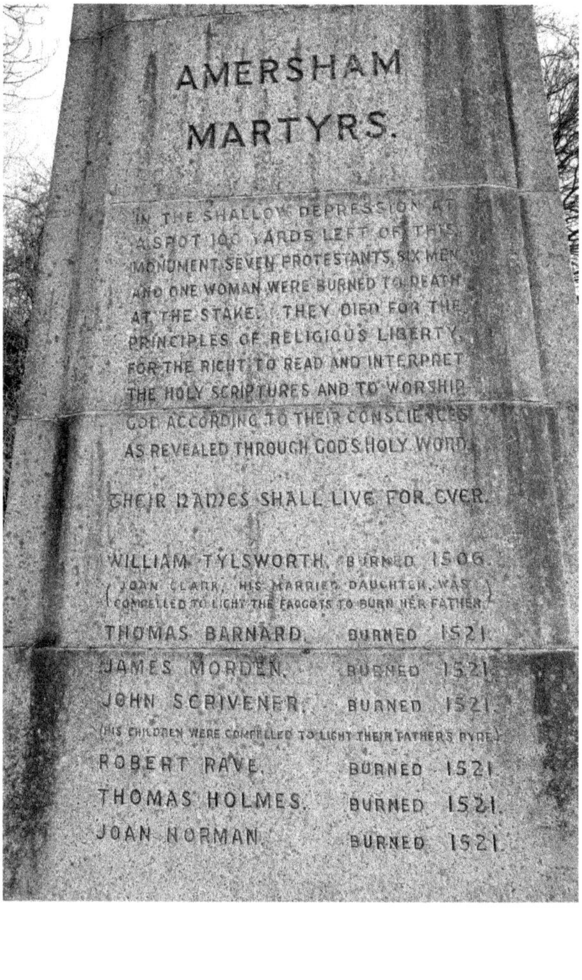

Martyrs Memorial.

each was burned at the stake. The most savage and heartbreaking of the executions was that of John Scrivener. His young children were forced to light their father's fire.

Thomas Harding, the last of the Lollard martyrs, was burned at Chesham in 1532. As the flames licked higher and the poor man writhed in pain one of the horrified spectators mercifully took pity on the wretched soul and threw a log at him that 'dashed out his brains', sparing him the prolonged agony of his fiery end.

In 1931 a memorial in the shape of a giant granite obelisk was erected on a hill overlooking Amersham to commemorate those who had suffered for their religious beliefs. It stands just 100 yards from where their execution pyres were lit, and looks over a town and countryside mostly unchanged since the sixteenth century, a final view which must have lingered in the eyes and minds of those martyrs back in a savagely intolerant time.

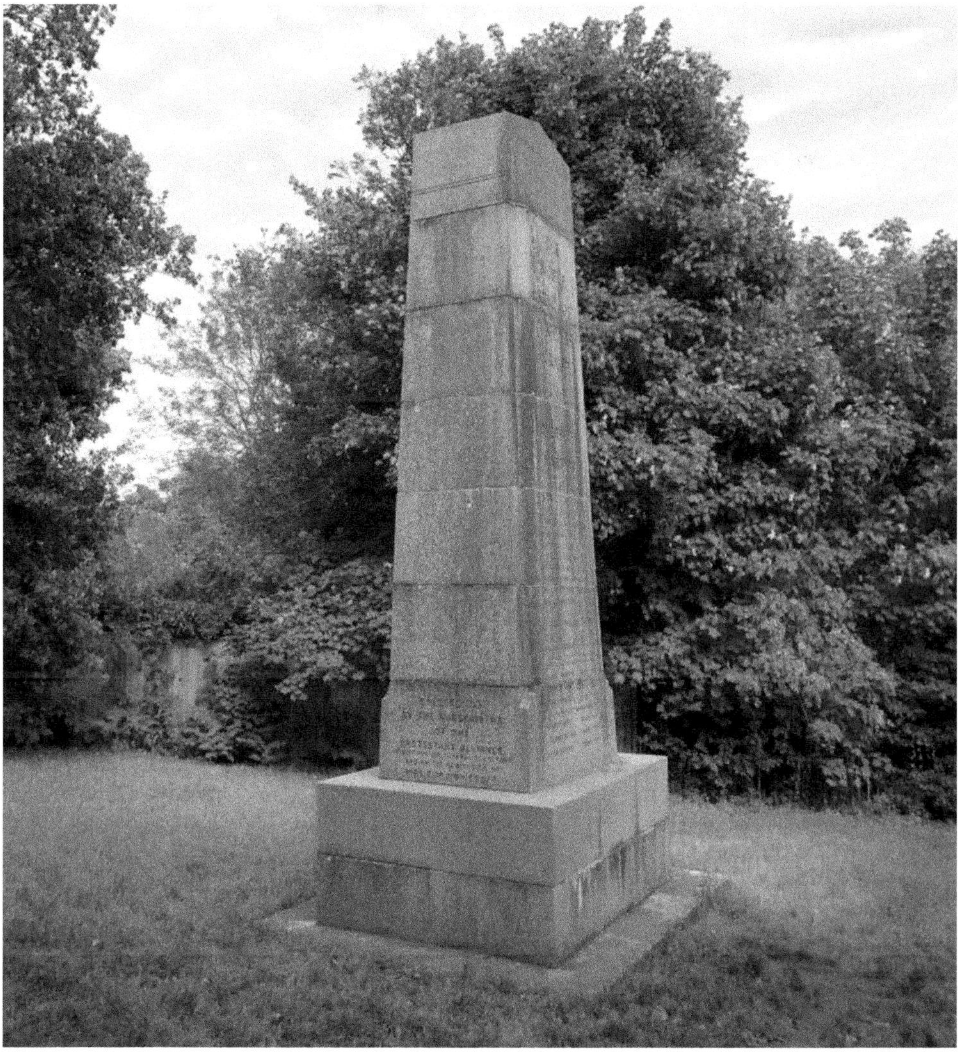

The Martyrs Memorial at Amersham.

The Strange Case of Noble Edden's Murder

Noble Edden was a fine, handsome young man who, in 1828, worked some land near Long Crendon where he had established a small nursery and took his produce to sell every market day in Aylesbury. His land lay on high ground which commanded far-reaching views of the surrounding countryside. One day he caught sight of a movement in the fields below. Two men were moving towards a flock of sheep. From their behaviour and the way they warily moved towards the animals Edden was in no doubt they were up to no good. What's more, even from his high distant vantage point, the nursery worker recognised the two men. He was shocked as he watched them move in among the sheep and kill one of the flock.

Soon after, the theft was discovered and the area was buzzing with speculation as to who might have carried out the crime. In 1828 sheep stealing was considered a most serious offence, which carried the death penalty or transportation. Noble Edden was well aware of this, but he was torn: should he give up the men to the authorities or remain quite? His word would have seen the men swing, but he didn't want their deaths on his conscience.

Nonetheless he felt that justice ought to be done in some way or another. Curiously, despite his misgivings about reporting the theft, Edden took to letting the two culprits know what he had observed. Every time he met the men he looked at them knowingly and then, bizarrely, commenced bleating like a sheep, 'Baa, Baa, Baa!' If he met them in the village, inn or on the road, it was 'Baa, Baa, Baa!' The two men ignored him, but they could hardly fail to realise that Edden knew of their crime, and that one word from him would be their end.

What is puzzling is that Noble seemed to be ignorant or unconcerned of his own predicament. Men who were willing to steal and kill sheep, and were desperate to save themselves from the hangman, were also capable of silencing the one person who could put the rope around their neck instead. One day, returning from Aylesbury market, Edden came across a man walking to Haddenham and he offered him a lift. The man recalled later that Noble had been in an agitated state and said he had a premonition that something terrible was going to happen to him. Meanwhile back in the kitchen of their cottage, Mrs Edden suddenly had an awful feeling that something bad had befallen her husband. In a paranormal vision she saw him being attacked by a man wielding a heavy hammer. She ran out in to the street crying out 'Dear God my husband is being murdered.' Her neighbours, alarmed at her distress, tried to calm her, but she insisted it was so. Noble Edden did not return home that night and later next day his body was found in a field near Haddenham. He had been beaten over the head, and his skull was crushed in.

At the inquest the following week a verdict of 'murder by persons unknown' was returned, and the body was given back to Mrs Edden. The moment the corpse was over the threshold the distraught widow called for the man she had seen kill her husband in the vision to come and lay his hand on the body. In those still superstitious days it was felt that, if a murderer touched the body of his victim blood would flow from the corpse's mouth and ears and the face would change colour – hence the saying 'murder will out'. The accused, a man named Tyler, refused the invitation. Several months passed and no one had been charged with the murder; however, suspicion began to fall on Tyler, and an accomplice by the name of Sewell. Yet the two men could hardly be arrested on the evidence of Mrs Edden's hysterical vision. During this time Noble Edden's son took over his father's business. Returning from Aylesbury one dark night he was set upon by two rogues. The young Edden fought them off, but the two attackers were heard to say 'We will do you the same as we did your old father.' It was too dark for the men's faces to be seen but Noble's son recognised the voices as Tyler and Sewell.

Sewell was Arrested on 16 August 1829 and charged with murder, but on what evidence is unclear. He was committed to Aylesbury Gaol where he made a statement implicating Tyler. Sewell's accomplice was arrested three days later and both men were brought before magistrates. Mrs Edden related her account of seeing her husband murdered in a vision and the man who had struck him was undoubtedly Tyler. Sewell's

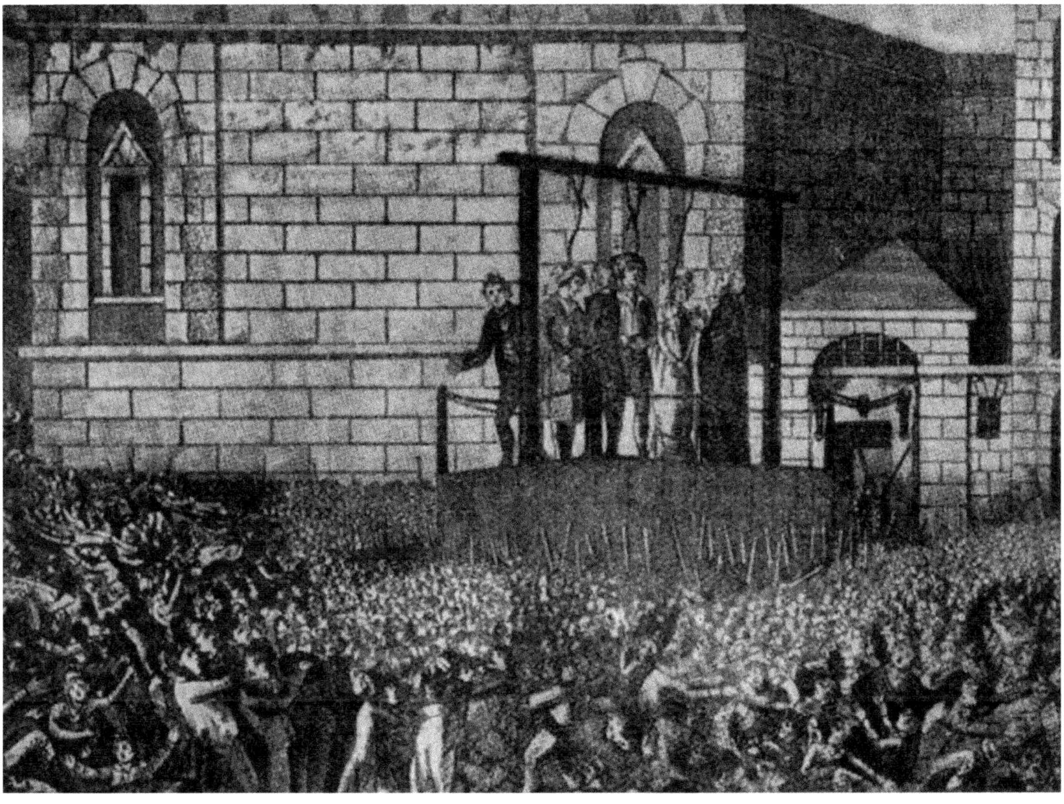

Public hanging.

statement was then read out in which he said he had seen Tyler strike Edden with the hammer. For some reason the magistrate did not believe him.

Sewell's mother was called and was of the opinion that her son could not have committed such a terrible crime because he was an idiot. Imbecility ran in the family, and she had twenty-four children to prove it so. Meanwhile Tyler continued to plead his innocence, and incredibly the magistrate believed him. Sewell's evidence was considered unworthy and Tyler was released. The freed man went quickly home to Thame, dressed himself in gaily coloured ribbons and danced at the doors of everyone who had testified against him. Sewell was brought before the court a week later and discharged, even though the magistrate had told him that he was a liar. However, the moment he stepped outside the court he was re-arrested for stealing a chicken and he was back in Aylesbury Gaol. He was sentenced to fourteen months' transportation, but in an attempt to save his skin he said he would at last speak the truth about the murder of Edden. Incredibly he was believed this time when he said Tyler was the murderer, but it didn't help him in his bid to be acquitted. Both men were sent to trial.

Sewell played the idiot whilst in the dock, repeatedly waving to the gallery. Tyler declared that he was as innocent as a newborn baby. Both were found guilty of Noble Edden's murder. On 8 March 1830 5,000 people gathered outside Aylesbury Gaol to witness the execution. Sewell kept up his imbecilic games, calling out 'Goodbye, Mr Taylor, I am about to die and go to heaven.' Tyler trembled with fear. He declared his innocence. Before he could say any more the cap was drawn over both men's faces and the next moment the trapdoor opened.

Phantasms of the Living

In 1936, shortly before his death, eminent English ghost story writer M. R. James was asked this question by his friend, Irish diplomat Sir Shane Leslie: 'Seeing as he had written better ghost stories than any man living, what were his thoughts on the reality of the paranormal.' He replied, 'Think on it, some of these things are so, but we do not know the rules.'

James was right: the first reported instance of a poltergeist occurred in what is now modern Germany 800 years before the birth of Christ, and in AD 100 the Roman scholar Pliny the Younger recorded what is regarded as the first story of a ghost hunt in a haunted house in Athens. Yet, 2000 years on psychical research has failed to fully understand why and how paranormal incidents occur. If we are to comprehend what M. R. James calls the 'rules', it would seem that we must look beyond the traditional

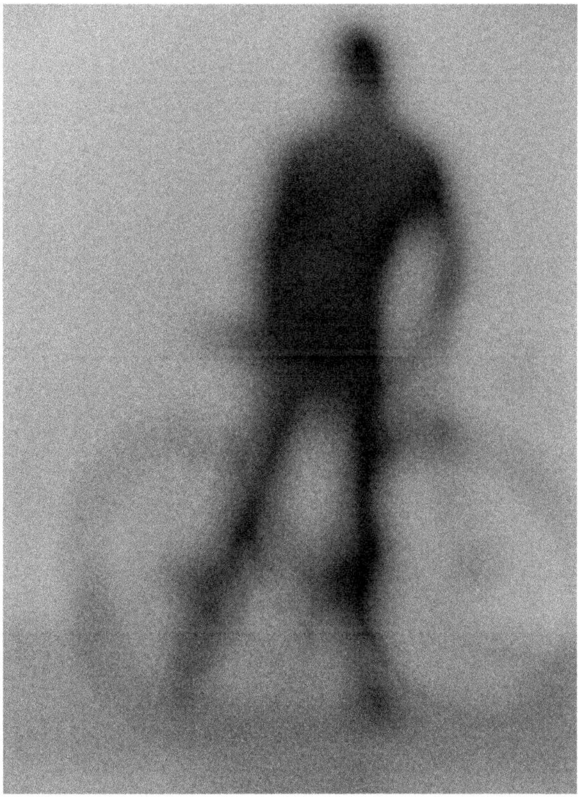

Phantasm of the living.

realm of the supernatural with its vocabulary of ghosts, hauntings and Earth-bound spirits which go bump in the night, and ask if the paranormal has just as much to do with the living as it does with the dead. Can a ghost or a supernatural incident be a vision of a future event, or indeed the apparition of a living person? The following account demonstrates this peculiar phenomenon.

Within the archives of the SPR there exist countless accounts of what are known as 'Phantasms of the living'. Sometimes referred to as crisis ghosts, they are apparitions which to all intents and purposes act and behave in the same manner one would expect the traditional spook to. They can materialise from nowhere, and just as suddenly vanish. Yet when viewed appear to be as solid and real as a flesh and blood human being. They are said to reveal their presence to friends and family members at the moment of death, signifying a final farewell. However, there are numerous other cases in which the vision of the 'phantom' or apparition is not on the verge of death but is indeed in the prime of a healthy life.

In 1988, a young secretary was on her way to a meeting at her office in Bletchley. A delayed start had put her behind schedule and when she encountered heavy morning traffic she realised she would be late. As the jam moved irritatingly slowly she got more and more frustrated. To go barely half a mile took ages. As the time ticked away she became increasingly stressed, and knowing she wouldn't make the meeting on time thought about turning around and heading back home. She eventually arrived at the office, flustered and tense some forty minutes later. As she entered the building she met

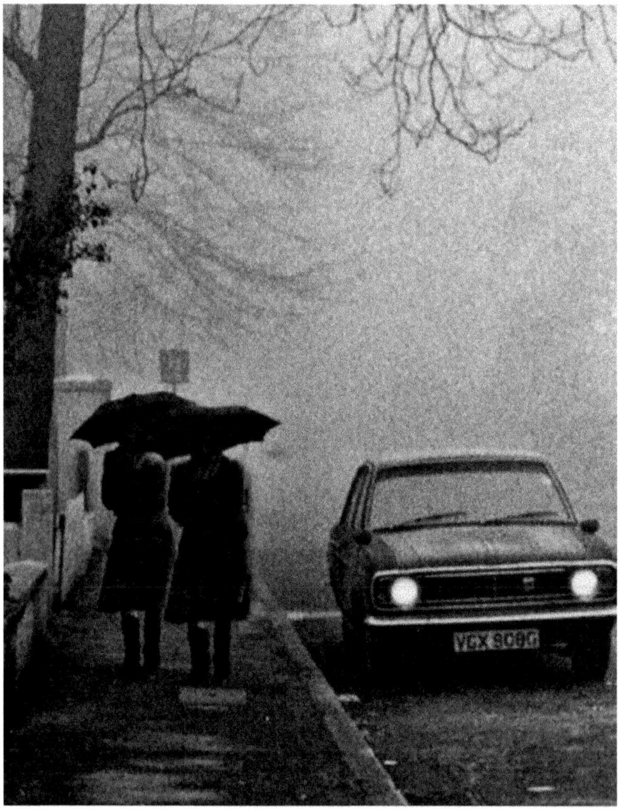

Sometimes some ghosts can turn out to be real people.

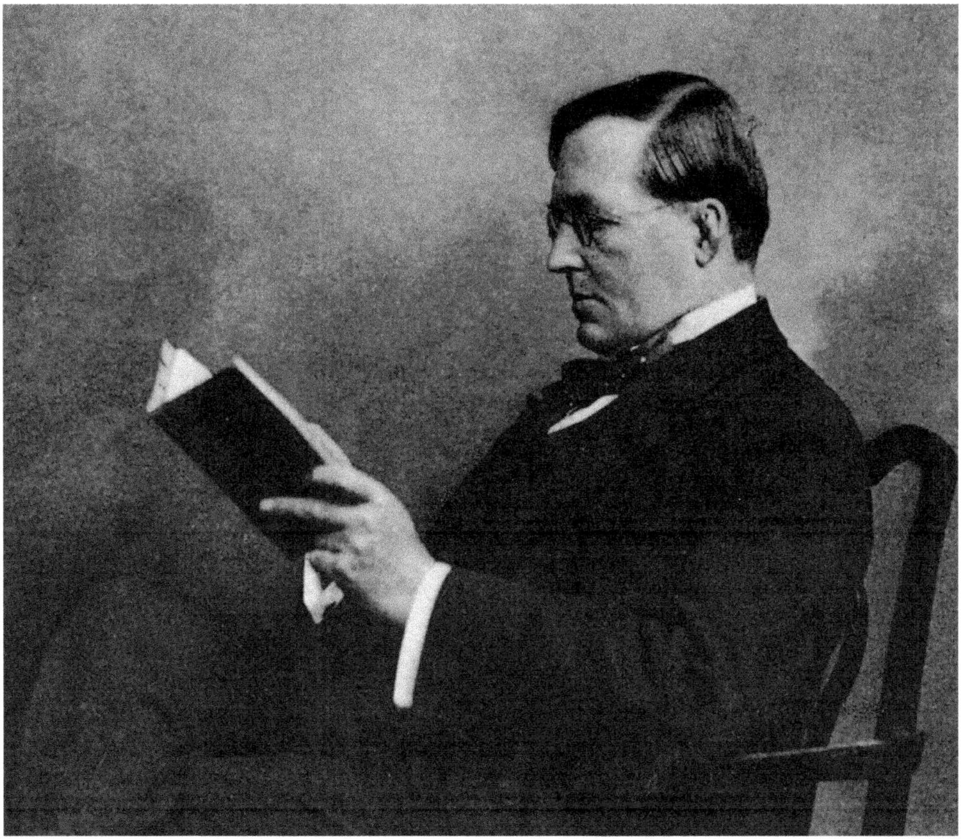

English ghost story writer M. R. James.

two colleagues who asked where she had gone to. The secretary misunderstood the question and replied that she had been stuck in traffic. 'No', the two men re-explained, 'fifteen minutes ago we saw you enter and then turn around and hurry back out.' She informed them that it could not have been her as fifteen minutes earlier she had been in her car miles from the office. However, they were insistent that they had earlier viewed her enter and leave the building.

Is it possible that the secretary, anxious and worried about missing the meeting, had in some way managed to telepathically transmit an image of herself into the office? Perhaps her thoughts on abandoning her trip and returning home had manifested in her being seen entering the building and hurrying back out. It would seem that the vision of the secretary is related, in some way, to the crisis apparitions of those who are near death. The fatally injured soldier's last thoughts are of his family and home, he needs and wants to be with them, and his image is seen by his loved ones walking up the garden path to the front door. The secretary needed and wanted to be at the meeting, and her colleagues saw an apparition of her enter the building.

The Haunting of Wycombe Station

On a chilly, misty night in 1986 a British Rail employee was waiting for a train on platform three of High Wycombe station. The station was empty and quiet, yet as he stood under the cold glow of the platform lamps, he heard the sound of approaching footsteps. However, they were not on the platform, but were coming from the ballast down on the track. He looked over onto the track expecting to see a railway worker walking along the line, but was astonished to see that the track was completely empty. As he listened, he heard the disembodied crunching noises passing by below him. It is not only phantom footsteps crunching the ballast which have been reported at the station. The frantic footfalls of someone running down the platform have been heard on several occasions, but on investigation there is nothing to account for them.

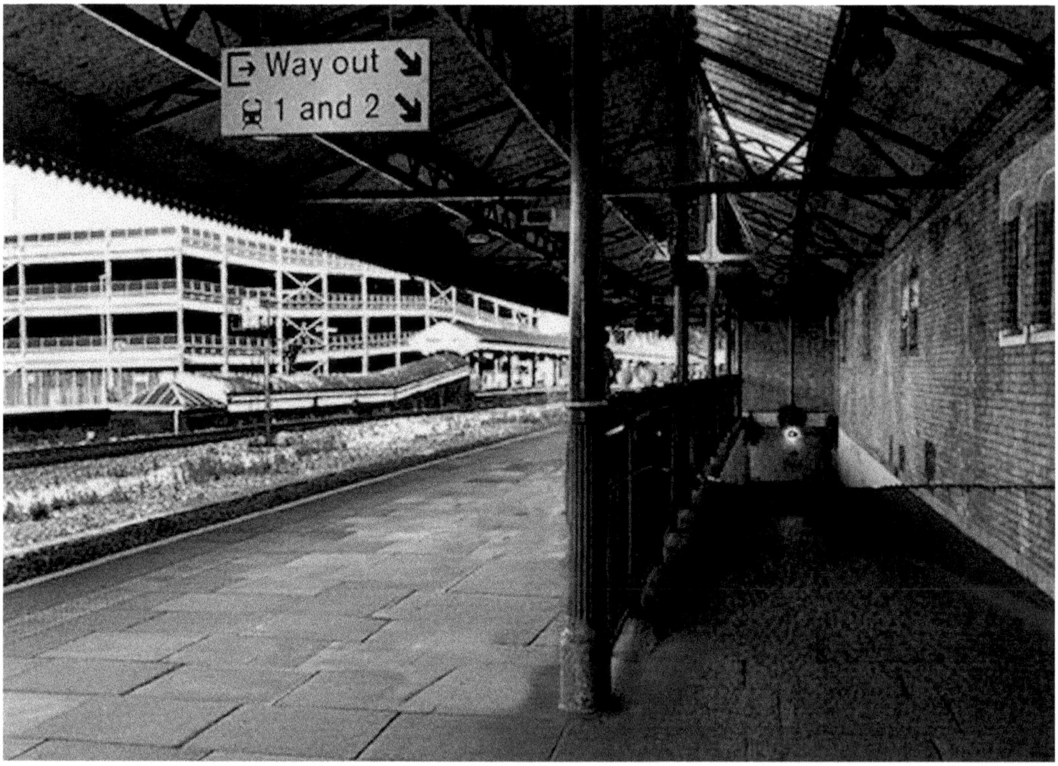

The haunted platform at Wycombe station.

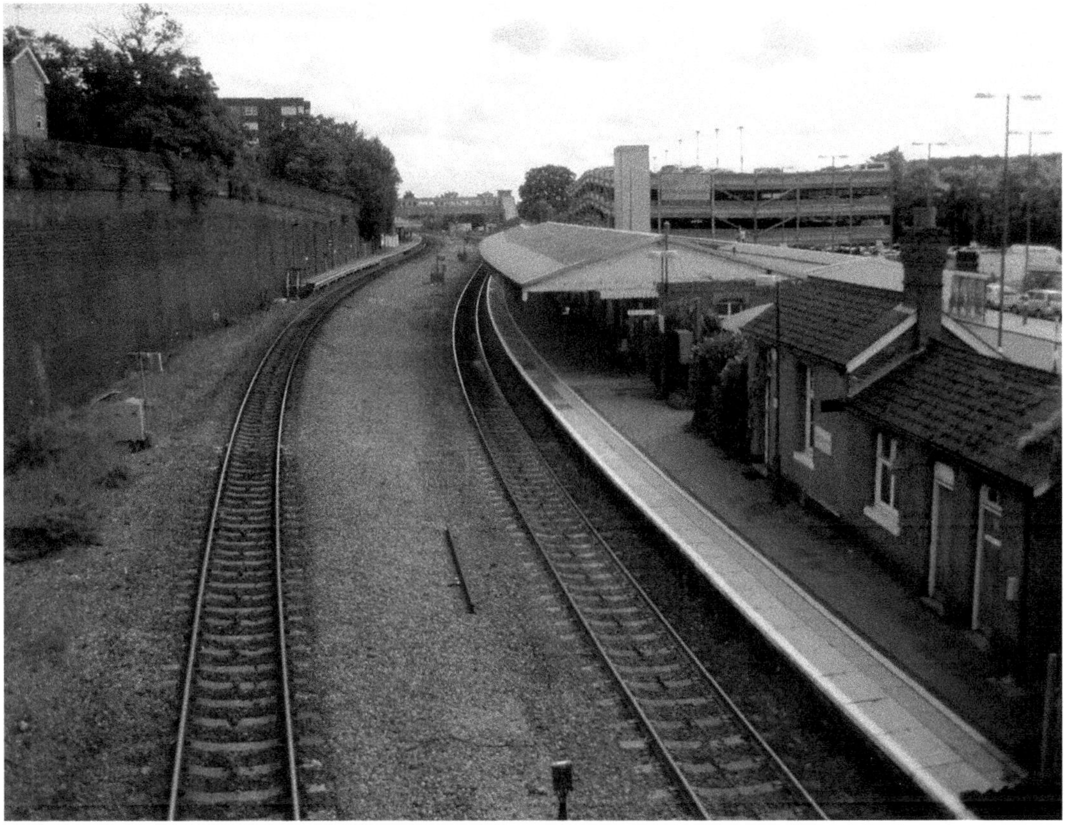

High Wycombe station.

The Miracle of Marlow

The phrase 'truth is stranger than fiction' is often applied to those incidents and episodes which leave the reader open-mouthed and scratching their head in disbelief. The following account demonstrates this only too well.

One morning in 1832 a resident of Marlow said goodbye to his wife as he went off to work. He told her he would return that evening and that they would enjoy a good dinner together. The man's wife was happy, healthy and in good sprits as she bade farewell to her husband. However, when the man returned that evening he was surprised to find the house empty and his wife not at home. Soon, distraught and

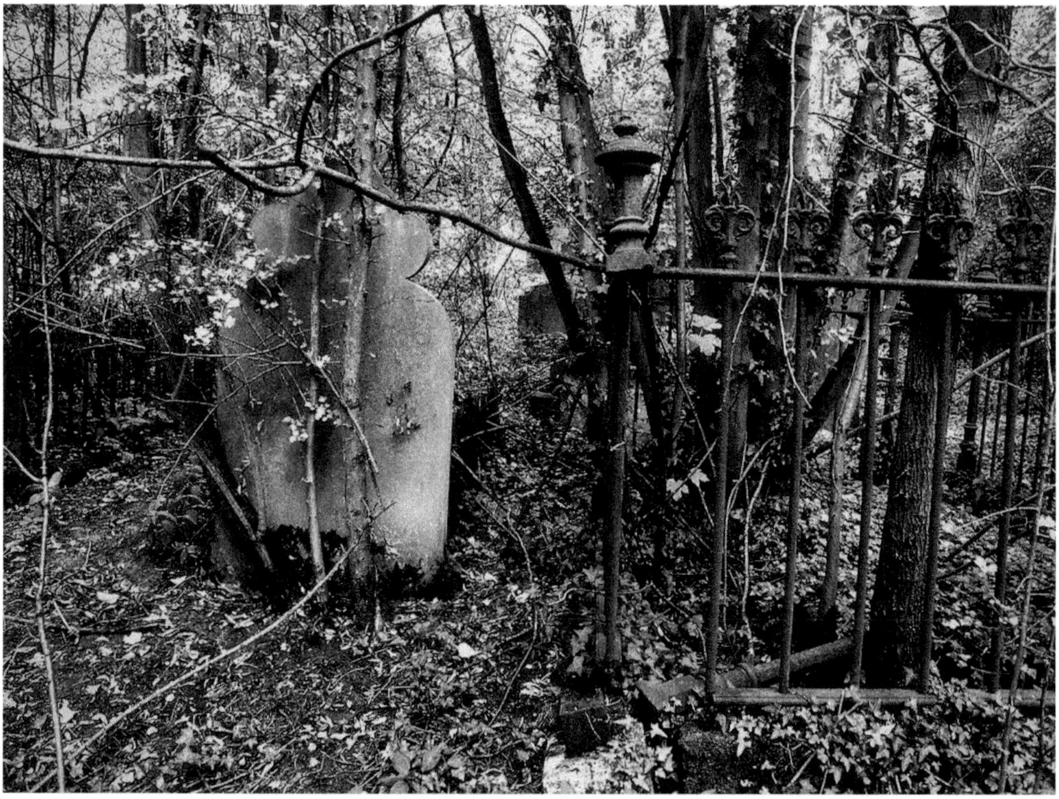

The miracle of Marlow, where a woman was saved from the grave.

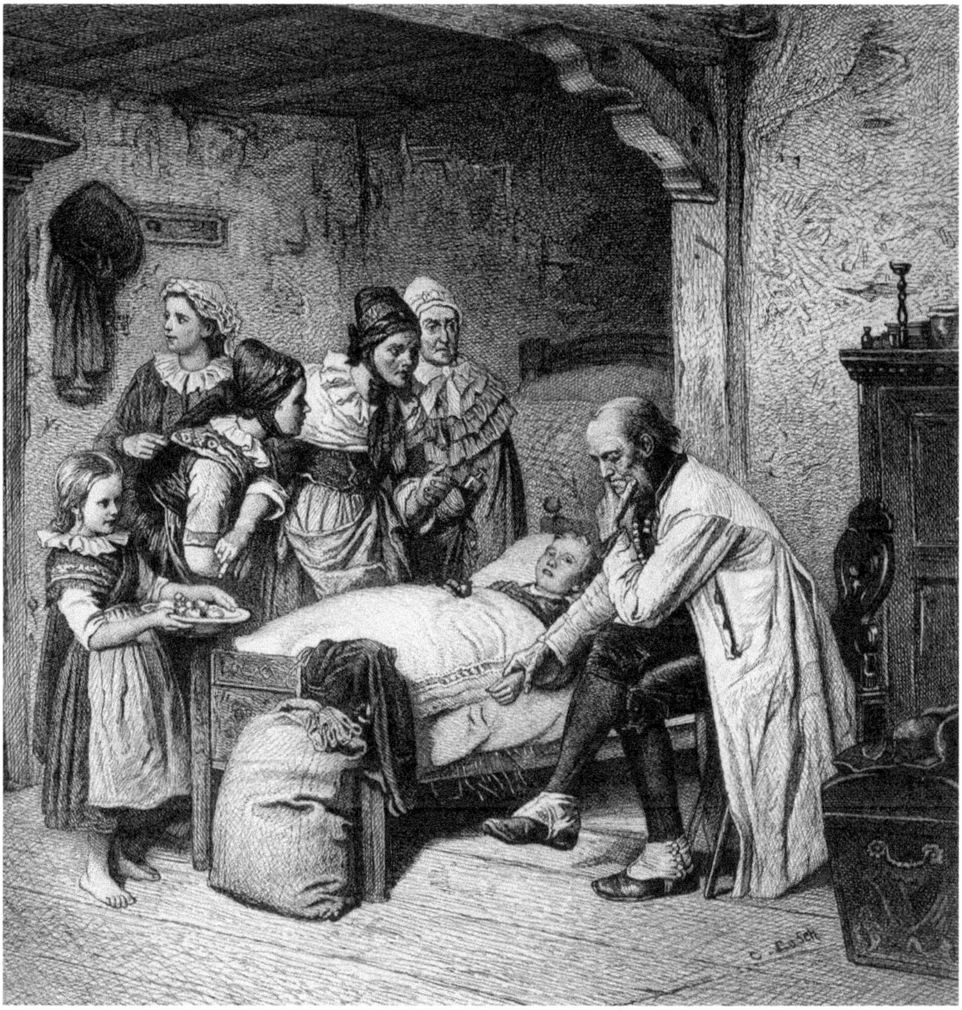

The scourge of cholera.

anxious, neighbours came to the man's home to tell him the devastating news that his wife had died that morning and had to be hurriedly buried.

The distressed man could not believe that his true love had been taken from him so quickly and without warning. He said that he could hear her voice calling to him from the grave, and in anguish rushed to the churchyard where she had been laid and desperately dug down to the coffin and opened the lid. To his astonishment he perceived signs of life, which were soon confirmed when the woman sat up in the coffin to the great joy of her husband. The woman recovered and both returned home, much to the amazement of the locals. Incredibly, that same night she gave birth to a child.

Phantom Footsteps at Beaconsfield Station

Ghosts can crop up in the most unlikely locations and situations. But there are certain places and sites where it would seem that the paranormal and the venue go hand in hand, such as ruined castles, stately homes, graveyards and old churches. For me, one location which seems tailor made for hauntings are Britain's railways – miles upon miles of lonely trackways, tunnels, bridges, signal boxes and, of course, stations.

When one considers the hard nature of the railways, the toil and graft that went into their construction, and the potential for calamity and disaster in their operation, it is no wonder that life wasn't very permanent for the men working on the permanent way.

Beaconsfield station is located on the Chiltern line between London and Birmingham. Readers will have to imagine the location back in the 1950s – a time of transition from steam to diesel-powered trains, semaphore to lighted signalling and wooden platforms – when this story takes place.

One misty night porter Harry Standon was working the late duty. The last train had left and the platforms were empty under the cold glow of the station lamps. Standon had locked up the building, including the gate to platform one where the staffroom was situated. The porter made himself comfortable in the warmth of the room and sat back in his chair expecting a quite night.

Some moments later he heard the sound of heavy boots crunching on stone. He naturally assumed that a maintenance man had turned up to carry out work on the track, and waited for him to call to the porter to open the gate to the platform. But no one called out. As Standon listened he heard the footsteps continue. Now they sounded on wooden boards as they approached the staffroom, yet this was impossible as the porter had securely locked the gate. The porter reasoned that if it wasn't a maintenance man it had to be a lost passenger whom he had inadvertently locked in.

The puzzled Standon grabbed his lantern and went out to investigate, but there was no one to be seen. The station was eerily silent. He searched all the rooms, including the toilets, but could find nothing to account for the footsteps. He knew he was totally alone on the station on a dark and misty night. Even so, he returned to the staffroom and locked the door.

Despite his odd experience, the porter reasoned that there had to be a rational explanation for the footsteps. When it was time for him to again work the night shift he had almost forgotten the puzzle of the phantom walker.

However, on another misty night after the last train had departed the porter once again locked up the station and settled himself in the warmth of the staffroom. After a while he once gain heard footsteps approaching along the platform. He immediately sat up and listened. The footfall came slowly on and, much to Standon's terror, stopped outside the staffroom. He looked at the door expecting at any moment it would be flung open, but all remained silent. After some time, much to his relief, he heard the footsteps carry on down the platform and onto the track. The porter mustered his courage and rushed outside shining his lantern down on to the tracks. Once again there was no one in sight. The shaken man was to later learn that other staff members who worked the night shift had also experienced the phantom footsteps.

As in all similar stories some form of explanation comes forward which may or may not account for the haunting. It is believed that some years before a plate layer working on the line at Beaconsfield during a windy, stormy night was killed when he failed to hear the approach of a diesel locomotive.

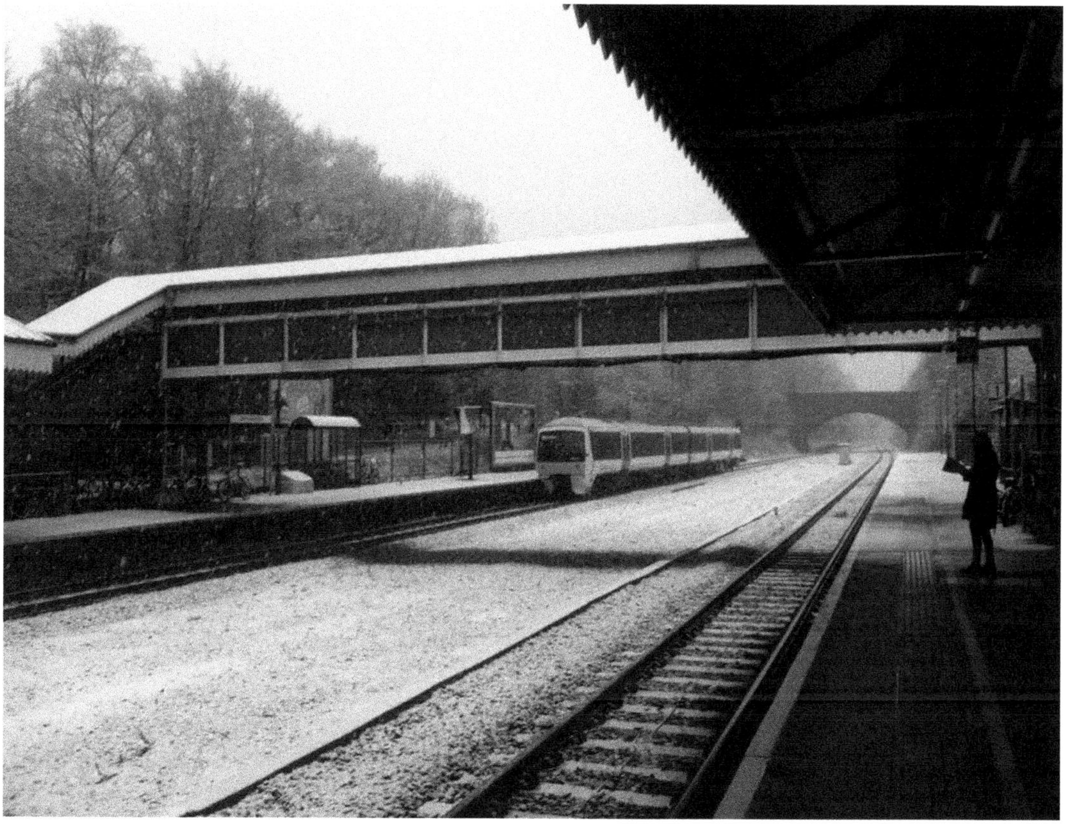

Haunted Beaconsfield station.

Ancient Ghosts at Chenies

Chenies Manor is a Grade I listed Tudor building owned by the Dukes of Bedford for several hundred years. Although it remains a private residence, the house and gardens are open to the public and are also used as a filming and wedding venue. The house was the ancestral seat of John Russell, 1st Earl of Bedford (*c.* 1485–1555), a favourite minister of Henry VIII who visited the house with Anne Boleyn, their daughter Elizabeth (subsequently Elizabeth I), and later with Catherine Howard. The adjacent church of St Michael's contains the Bedford Chapel where John Russell and later members of his family, the various Earls and Dukes of Bedford, and their wives, are interred.

The manor house became know publicly as a haunted building in 1956 shortly after it was sold by the Russell family to Lt-Col Alistair Macleod Matthews, a British

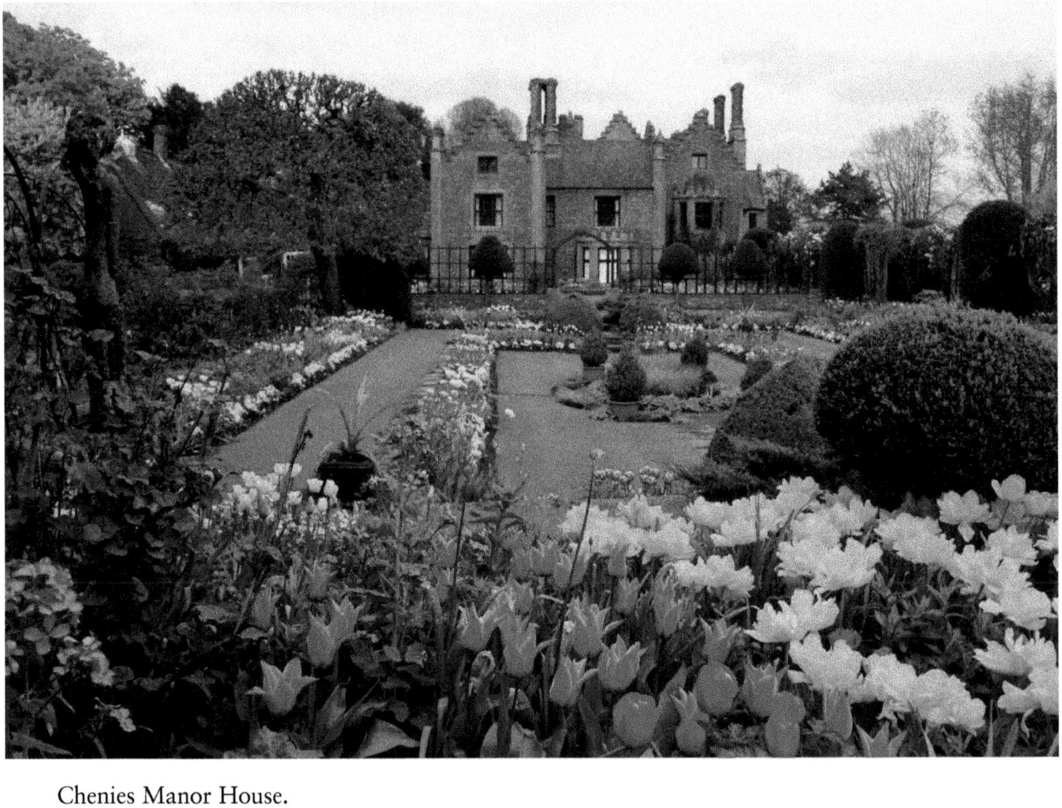

Chenies Manor House.

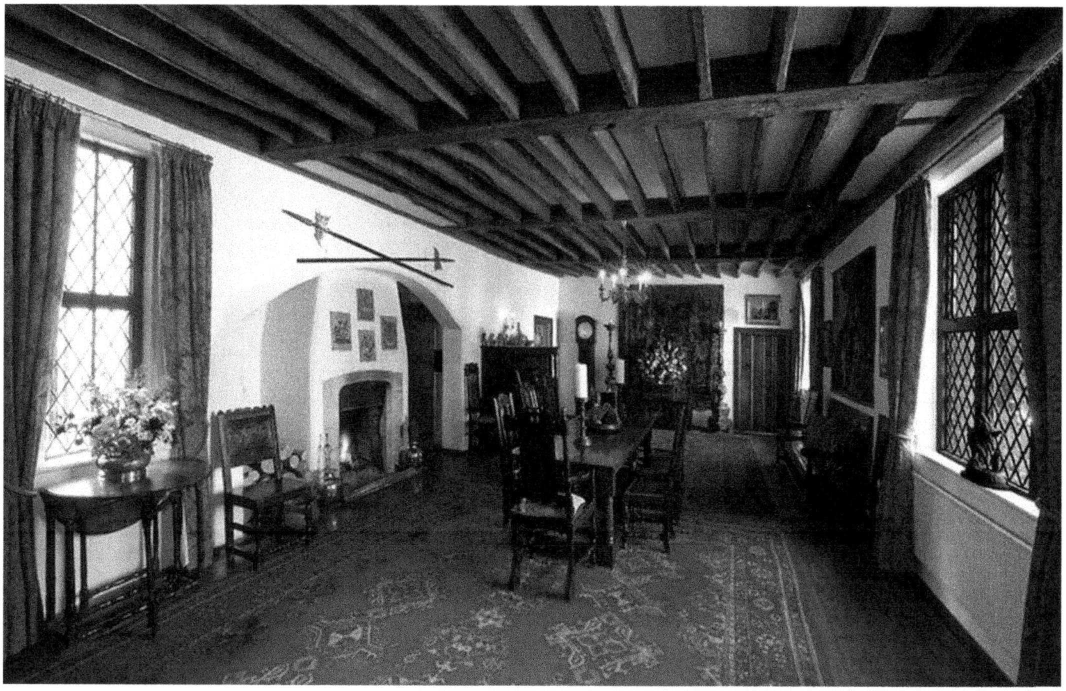

Chenies interior.

Petroleum company official, and his wife, Elizabeth. The couple told the *Evening Standard* that two nights after moving into the house from their flat in Lancaster Gate they were awakened by the sound of creaking floorboards and heavy measured footsteps. These emanated from a small room adjacent to a larger bedroom in which it was known that Elizabeth I had slept in during the summer of 1570. On investigation nothing was found to account for the sounds. It has been suggested that these footsteps, which were heard by Lt-Col and Mrs Matthews on several occasions, are those of Charles I, who was kept under arrest at Chenies during the time it was occupied by Cromwell's troops. A former priest hole, discovered behind brickwork in a bedroom known at one time as the Pink Room, is also associated with ghostly activity, in this case cyclical phenomena reported to occur on 9 September when in the past the door and windows have been found to have mysteriously opened by themselves. Chenies Manor was one of several sites visited by members of the Ghost Club during its centenary year in 1962 during the Peter Underwood era.

Solitary Ghosts

On a sultry, overcast day in August 1987, thirty-eight-year-old Sara Osborne took her usual walk across the fields near Tylers Green, close to the town of High Wycombe. Here the paths fan out in different directions, but Sara continued on a circular route. The fields and footpaths were unusually empty of other walkers, and Sara recalls that the grey day seemed strangely still and silent.

She had almost completed her walk and was nearing a farm when she looked ahead and saw a figure standing motionless on the path some 100 yards away. The person appeared to be an extremely tall man dressed in a long black coat which hung down below his knees. He wore what seemed to be white gloves, and his left hand hung by his side whilst his right, positioned at his midriff, pointed towards her.

His whole attire seemed out of place and completely wrong for the sticky, humid day.

However, as Sara stared at the strange figure she realised something which made her go cold and distinctly queasy: the head of the man seemed to be abnormally small as if it had been shrunk, like the head of a baby planted onto the neck of an adult. There were no features: no eyes, nose or hair. It was just like a small stump protruding from the man's shoulders. The whole scene was disturbingly weird, and she wondered if the figure was some kind of optical illusion brought about by the humid atmosphere. The thought of continuing in the direction of the man and passing him was extremely disagreeable to her.

She turned and made her way back along the path which led to the main road of the village. Before passing out of the fields she reluctantly looked back to see if the figure had chosen to follow her. Much to her relief, and surprise, he was nowhere to be seen.

However, Sara's curiosity compelled her to retrace her steps partway back into the field to see if she could catch sight of the strange person. But there was no one there.

She returned home unsettled and disturbed by the incident, and was at a complete loss as to an explanation. The whole episode felt real and uncanny enough for her to flee the scene and, for weeks after, give her many sleepless nights. Following her strange encounter she refrained from taking her solitary walk across the fields, and it took some time for her to once again feel safe enough to do so, and only in the company of friends.

The experience of Sara Osborne is not only extraordinary and bizarre, but eerily creepy, and one wonders in to what file such apparitions should be catalogued: ghosts, spectres, phantoms of the living, doppelgangers, evil spirits?

Although hard to classify, such visions are not without precedent. In the early hours of a January morning in 1976, twenty-three-year-old Brian Perkins from Aylesbury was on his way to work at a local bakery near to his home. It was 4.00 a.m. on a cold, damp morning, and despite it being in a busy part of the town the streets were eerily deserted. As he passed by a church on his way to the main road he momentarily looked in the direction of the graveyard, and to his surprise and utter shock, standing on a patch of grass some way within the yard was a figure resembling an extremely tall skeleton.

Perkins instantly stopped in his tracks trying to comprehend what he was seeing. The motionless figure was half illuminated by the feeble yellow neon from the surrounding street lamps. At first the young man thought he was the victim of a practical joke, and soon the revellers would reveal themselves and take off laughing. But that didn't happen. Without warning the skeleton figure began to move towards Perkins – not so much walking but gliding very slowly. The young man felt unable to flee as his terror seemed to have prevented any bodily movement. Then, whilst Perkins looked on, the figure, as it closed, gradually began to fade away into the shadows of the churchyard.

Wanting to ensure that he was not being set up, the young man, with admirable courage, entered the graveyard towards the area where the figure had disappeared, but there was nothing to indicate what he had witnessed or why it had vanished. Perkins then took off, and ran as he had never ran before to his workplace.

As to be expected, his relating of the experience to workmates was met with the expected laughs and ridicule. Over the following years Brian Perkins would come to pass that churchyard on numerous occasions, day and night, but never again encountered the figure of the skeleton.

What are we to make of such uncanny encounters? Could they be some form of illusion we have yet to understand or is there a more sinister aspect to their manifestation? These incidents seem to be random, isolated supernatural episodes which appear have no reason or purpose, unless it is to alarm and frighten, which they certainly do. Significantly, each occurrence was never independently reported

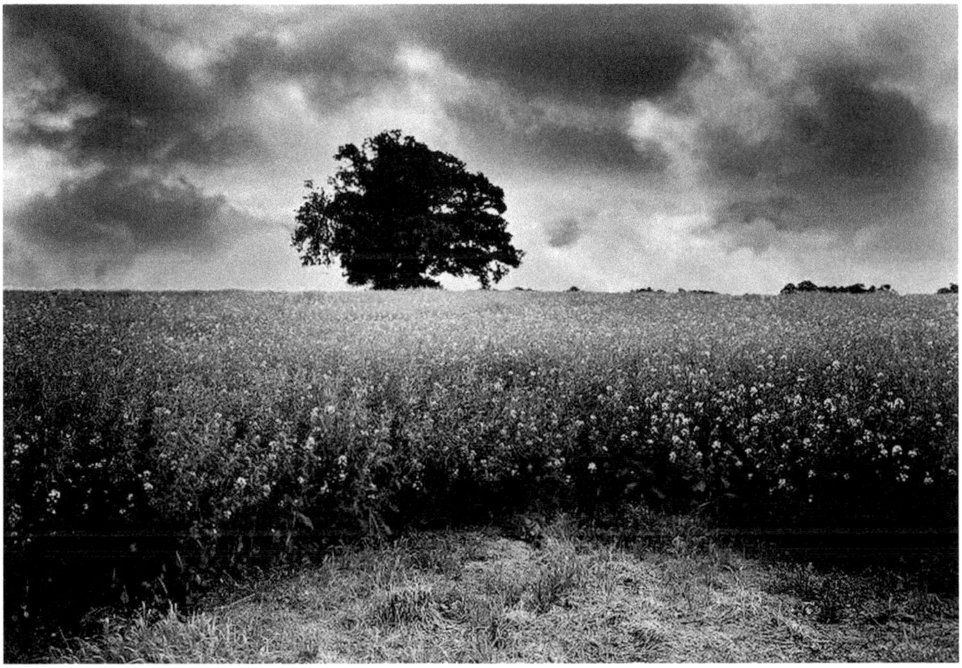

The eerie summer landscape near Tylers Green and Penn.

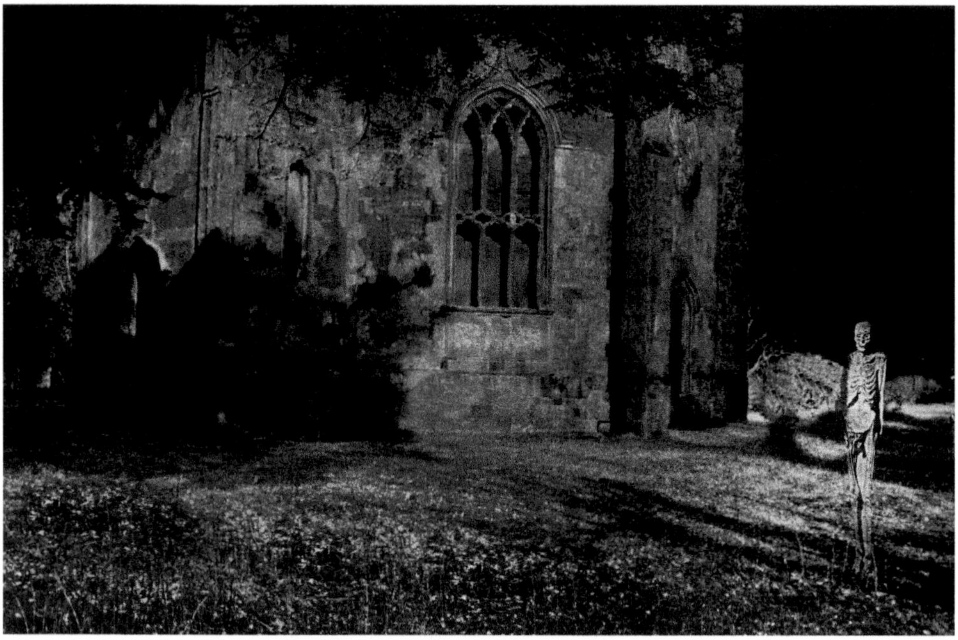

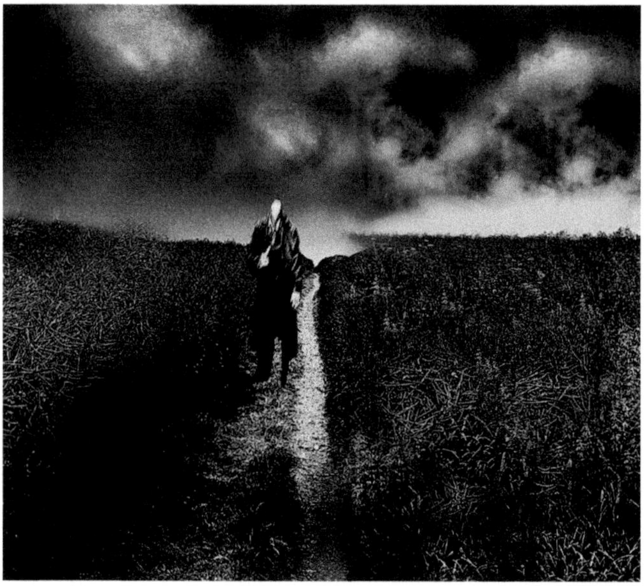

Above: The terrifying apparition witnessed by Brian Perkins in an Aylesbury churchyard.

Left: A representation of what Sarah Osbourne saw on her walk.

previously or subsequently, and for both Osborne and Perkins it was their one and only encounter with the paranormal.

Such encounters seem to be psychical blips; mysterious abnormalities which remain apart from the main body of paranormal phenomena. Yet, that would seem to imply that the supernatural is bound by rules, and the episodes described are some kind of wayward paranormal anomaly, like a misbehaving child, which chooses to disobey the code.

Footsteps on the Stairs – How I Became a Ghost Hunter

The most frequently asked question put to paranormal researchers is perhaps an obvious one: 'How did you become a ghost hunter?' It is one which has often been inquired of me. The query would appear to require an easy enough reply. Yet, when the question is put a mental back-tracking begins as we recall the years and try to locate that moment, hour or day when we were snared by the subject and became intoxicated with a passion to discover more.

Of course, certain foundations have first to be in place. A curiosity with the mysteries of the world, and of how and why certain things happen is necessary. Yet, there must also be that decisive moment; that spark which ignites the senses and imagination and entices us down the path of discovery of our chosen field. For me it was when I was ten years old during the summer of 1966 when my family were living in an eighteenth-century house in Stockwell, South London.

One warm afternoon I returned home from school at around 4 p.m. to find the house empty. Letting myself in, I went and sat in the kitchen and read comics whilst I awaited the return of my grandmother. It was unusual for the house to be empty during the afternoon as my gran was normally at home and my dad, who was a shift worker, would be either asleep or getting ready to go to work.

As I sat in the kitchen I became aware that the house had become unnaturally still and quiet. The muffled sound of the traffic, and the shrieks and shouts of the other kids playing outside, seemed to have been deadened to silence, and once or twice I looked up from my comic to peer quizzically around the soundless room. Without warning my younger brother's toy robot, which he often left wherever he last played with it, clicked, whirred into life and began marching, Frankenstein fashion, across the floor towards me. The sudden breaking of the silence jolted me from my chair and I got up, went over and stopped the machine. There was no indication as to why it had inexplicably burst into life. I put it back in its box and returned to my seat, but not without a bewilderment.

Sometime later I suddenly heard a door at the top of the house close with a sharp slam, followed by footsteps. My immediate thoughts were that one of my brothers or my dad was at home and was now coming downstairs. And yet the sound of the descending footfall and the way they seemed to edge tentatively down each flight made me listen up. It didn't sound like my father's measured tread or the rushing eagerness of one of my brothers.

At once the thought came to me that it might be an intruder who had broken into the house and on hearing my return was now cautiously coming down the stairs to make their escape. The footsteps reached the bottom floor and seemed to halt outside

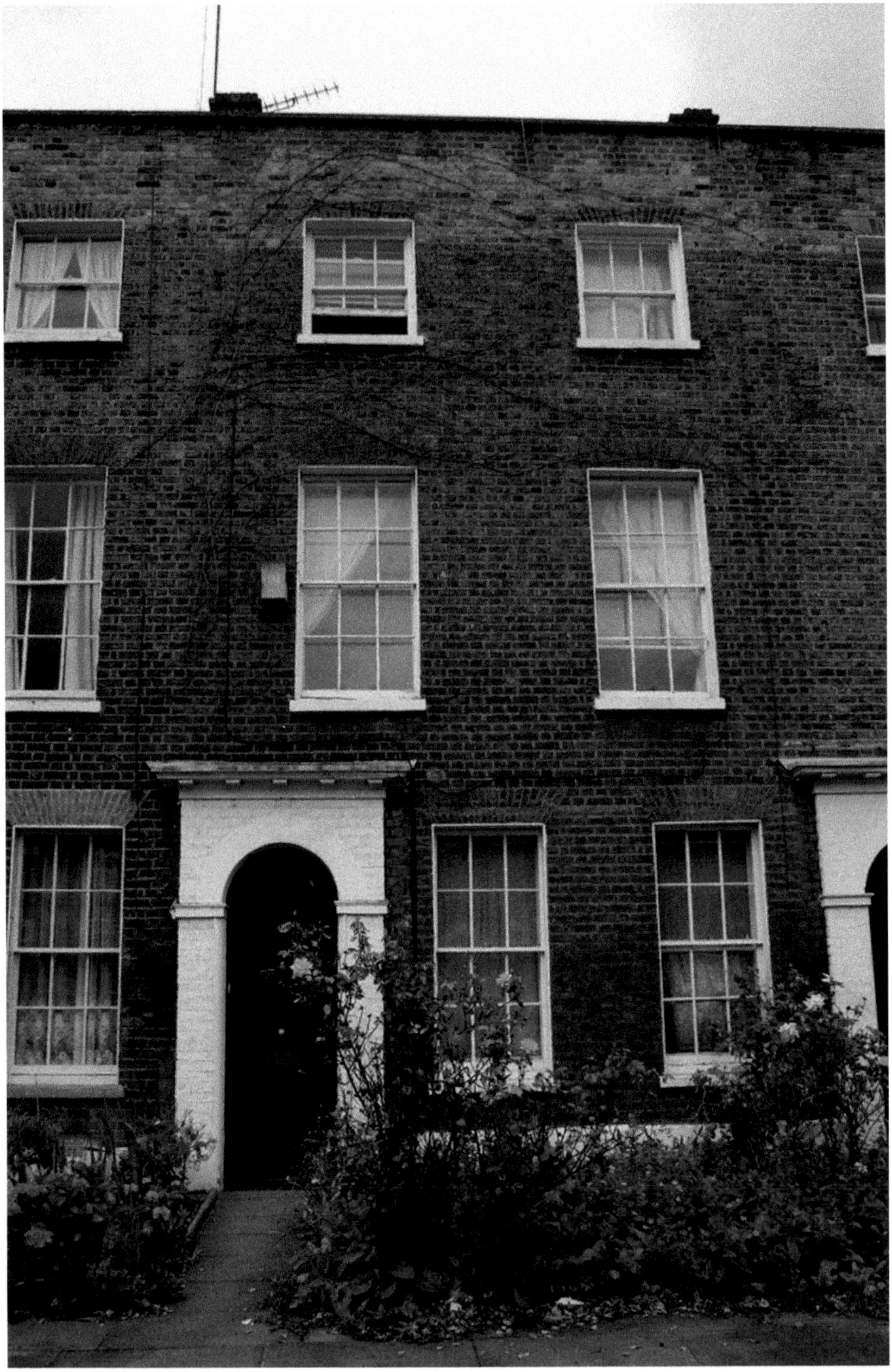

The author's childhood home in South London where he had his first paranormal experience.

the kitchen door. I sat transfixed, my eyes on the door, heart thumping, waiting to see who would enter.

At no time did I think the sounds were in anyway paranormal. I was certain that if I got up, went to the door and opened it I would be confronted by a large man with a stocking over his head and a crowbar in his hands. Yet, I didn't need to go over and open the door for, noiselessly and without warning, it swung open on its own. I sat upright in my chair half expecting to be bashed on the head by the intruder as he made his getaway. However, no one entered the kitchen. I eventually mustered enough courage to get up and go and look out into the hall. It was then that I realised that the sounds were not those of one of my family or the clumsy footsteps of a burglar. The hall and the first flight of stairs were empty. I panicked and bolted from the house, out through the kitchen door and into the garden. As I sat in the sunshine, too fearful to re-enter, a host of fanciful thoughts raced through my mind. What on earth was going on? What had I heard? Who had I heard? I was equally excited, bewildered and scared. Was it possible that I had heard a genuine ghost? Was our house haunted? And what would I see and hear if I went back inside and climbed to the top landing where I had earlier heard the door slam.

The arrival of my grandmother sometime later brought an air of normality to the situation and I went back, with some trepidation, into the kitchen. My cautious looks around the room, out in the hall and up the stairs, plus my initial reluctance to go and fetch something for my gran from her bedroom on the top floor of the house, brought from her a knowing look which seemed to say, 'Ah, so you have heard it too.'

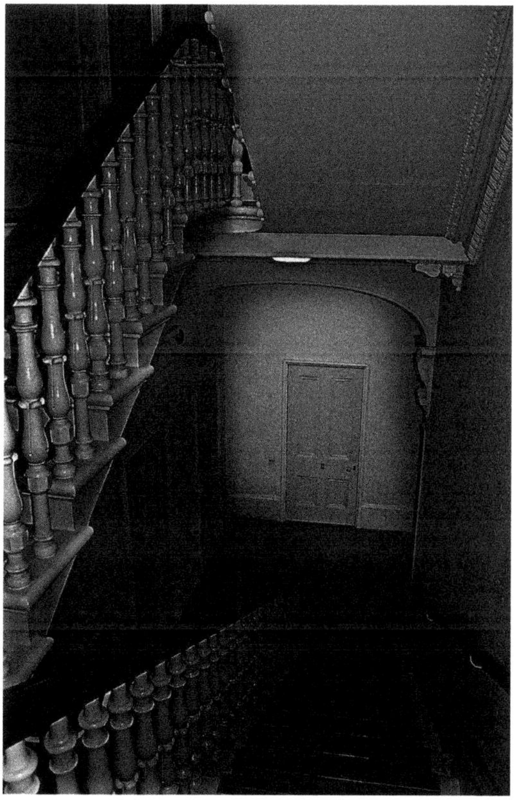

The footsteps came down the stairs and stopped outside the kitchen door.

Indeed my grandmother and my father had both experienced curious incidents in the house. I was later to learn that such was their concern that my brothers and me would become frightened if we learned of the strange things that were taking place that both tried to ignore what was happening. I, myself, refrained from sharing my experience with the rest of my family – partly because I feared ridicule from my brothers, but mainly because I was of the opinion that if I didn't refer or talk about it, it would soon be eliminated from my mind. However, it was my grandmother who eventually commented to my father one day, 'This is strange house, something is going on here.'

On certain days, alone in the house, she would hear footsteps in empty rooms and doors closing on their own. My father also experienced incidents he couldn't explain. During the night he would often hear the front door of the house open and close, followed by footsteps which would come along the hall and then ascend the stairs. The footsteps would pause outside his bedroom before continuing up to the top floor. Getting out of bed, he would open the door and emerge out onto the cold, dark landing to see if there was anything out of place and that we were all in our rooms asleep, which we were. The remaining years we spent in the house I never again experienced the footsteps phenomena or anything untoward. My grandmother and father continued to hear things which they couldn't explain, but treated the strange happenings with a shrug of the shoulders. It was a nonchalance which bordered on denial. They reasoned if they ignored the odd incidents, they would cease, which they gradually did.

We eventually moved on from Stockwell without finding a reason for the ghostly sounds. However, my family were to later learn that the subsequent tenants of the house also had the nerve-racking experience of hearing footsteps on the stairs during the night and doors opening and closing on their own.

That was many years ago. I inspire you to look again at the mysteries of the world and pose the question, 'Are there more things in Heaven and Earth?' I certainly hope so.

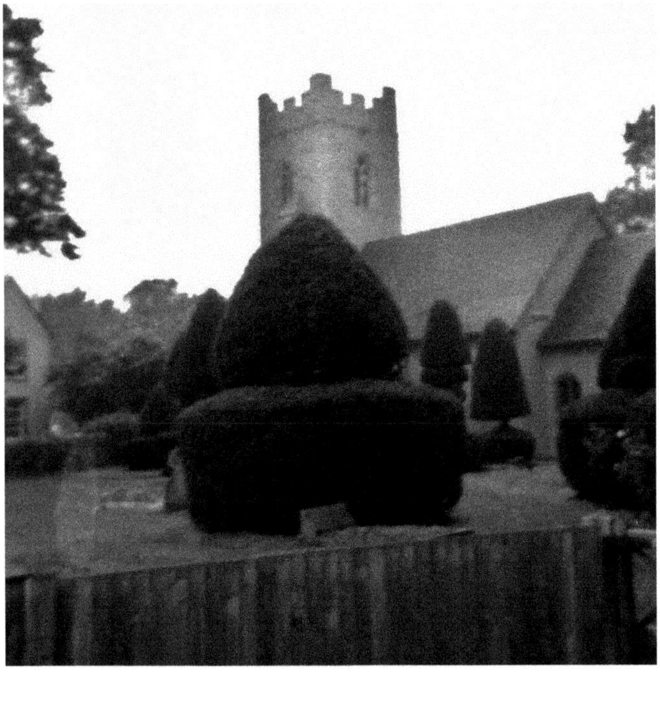

The photo which set the author on the road to ghost hunting – a strange figure snapped in the graveyard of Borley church in Essex, site of the infamous haunted rectory.

Acknowledgements

Once again, a big thank you to my wife, Sue, for her help and support during the writing of this book. Also to David Saunderton for help with photographs. A big thank you to my friend and colleague Paul Adams for the information on the Chenies case. And last, but by no means least, to all those departed souls who choose to remain among us: without you this book would not have happened.

About the Author

Eddie Brazil was born in Dublin in 1956 and later rised in South East London. He is a writer, photographer and paranormal investigator. He is the co-author, with Paul Adams and Peter Underwood, of *The Borley Rectory Companion* and *Shadows in the Nave: A Guide to the Haunted Churches of England*. In 2012, with Paul Adams, he wrote *Extreme Hauntings: Britain's Most Terrifying Ghosts*. He has also written on the *Bloody History of Buckinghamshire* and recently published *High Wycombe in 50 Buildings*.

He is also a guitarist, and in 1983 wrote the theme music to the British comedy movie *Expresso Splash O* which featured Gary Oldman and Daniel Peacock. Eddie lives with his wife and daughter in High Wycombe, Buckinghamshire.

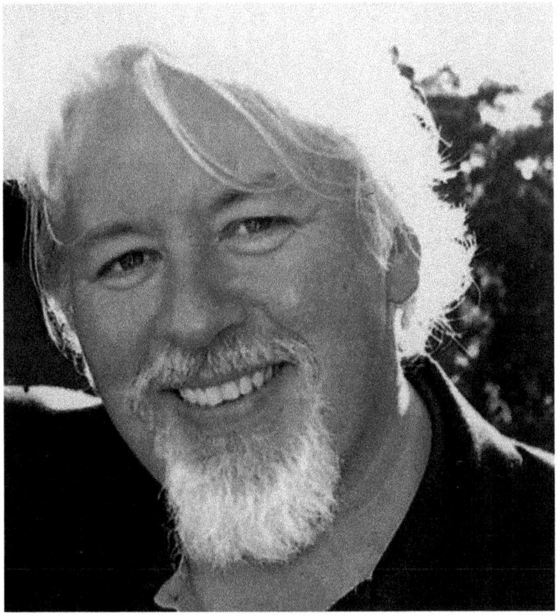